Scrawny Dog, Hungry Cat, and Fat Rat
A Tragedy for Children

Jerry Johnson

Illustrations by Bailey Cahlander

Typeset by Aaron Lurth

*Audre — remembering PJ days —
edit this! :) — Jerry*

Scrawny Dog, Hungry Cat, and Fat Rat - A Tragedy For Children

This book is dedicated to

C. Michael Shelton

1948-2013

A poet, gentle spirit, and

the best Cat a friend could want.

Table of Contents

Chapter 1   5

Chapter 2   13

Chapter 3   22

Chapter 4   31

Chapter 5   41

Chapter 6   53

Chapter 7   76

Chapter 8   89

Chapter 9   101

Chapter 10   116

Chapter 11   128

Chapter 1

How It All Started for Scrawny Dog, Hungry Cat, and Fat Rat

In the coldest part of a long dark night the three of them were huddled over an exhaust grate in the street: Scrawny Dog, Hungry Cat, and Fat Rat. They all looked pretty miserable, shivering in the wind and leaning back and forth to catch the warm air of the building's boiler room exhaust before the fan switched off. But they weren't unhappy. They agreed it was most fortunate that they should come upon this warm air a-blowing just when it seemed they would all freeze to the bone, wandering the streets on this winter night. It was a lucky thing. And so of course they got to talking about luck.

"I can never understand," said Hungry Cat, "Why it is always the luck of Rats to have the easy goin'."

"How's that?" asked Fat Rat, trying to remember a time when he had easy going.

"It seems plain as oatmeal to me," answered Cat, "that Rats always have good luck. If food is to be found, a Rat will find it, and even when everything is froze over solid, a Rat will find drinking water. Why, here tonight when it looked to be too cold for any hope, old Rat finds himself a hot air exhaust grate."

"Which is just as warm for Cat," said Rat.

Cat just sniffed a little sniff toward Rat and talked right on without slowing. "Even luckier is how Rats is never stoned nor sticked by children, or seldom squashed by cars, though plenty enough Cats and Dogs meet those ends."

"Plenty of Dogs do," agreed Scrawny Dog.

"So you see, Rat, we have to wonder about your Rat-luck," said Cat. "And both of us would be obliged if you would tell us why it's so."

Rat poked his skin-tail down between the wires of the exhaust grate and settled onto his furry fat behind. Being careful not to sit on his broken toe, he wished he felt half so lucky as Cat was feeling for him. Rat thought carefully for a few moments before saying anything, because a smart Rat will avoid back-talking a Cat whenever possible. Then he cleared his throat and started out slowly.

"Cat, you have an odd sense of luck, it seems to me," Rat said. "Most of what you're calling luck ain't luck at all – it's just Rattin'. That's the way things work out for Rats because of what they is. And what they is is prodent."

"You mean 'prudent'," said Dog.

"No, I mean 'prodent,' as in 'rodent'," Rat answered back. "So don't interrupt."

Rat turned to face Cat. "Now, as I was explaining, what you are calling good luck is just the way things work out for Rats because of what they is and what they do. You see, Dogs don't have that kind of luck because they are always Dogging themselves into trouble. And Cats don't have luck like Rats because – well, on account of they act like Cats."

Dog scratched his head with his back left foot like he had the worst confusion. "What are you talking about, Rat?"

"Why, it's most clear to me," continued Rat, "that Rats come by their good luck through avoiding all those things that Cats and Dogs do that cause their bad luck. Take Dogs, for instance. Now Dogs live in the street, oftener than not, and there is no luck in that, but they seem happy to do it, even where there's cars and trucks and buses zooming by like crazy.

"And Dogs are friendly to all kinds of folks and will walk right up with a wagging tail to say 'Hi there!' and make themselves feel friendly and welcome. Even your growling or barking Dog will strut right up to a person he don't know, a perfect stranger, and growl or bark without a thought about being careful.

"That is why Dogs is so often hit with poor treatment: they are not careful! They don't know how to act prodent," said Rat. "Why, I've known many a Dog that's been whipped to fractures by a kid who tempted him over with a big hunk of something good in one hand and a big stick in the other. Same with dogs that go out hunting, or chasing cars, or scaring chickens. More times than not, they won't be paying the least attention to their luck, and sooner or later it will cost them.

"That's how it is," said Rat. "If you fool around all the time, if you are not prodent, you're going to run into an awful amount of bad luck."

"Oh, piffle!" yelped Dog. "If you want to have a good time, you got to go do some fooling around."

"Just what I say," snapped Rat. "If you're looking for good times, you ain't looking out for bad times, which means you're too busy having fun for luck to come your way. And all Dogs are good-timers. Why a dog doesn't want to have a time unless it's going to be a good one. They're always running, always jumping, chasing this, barking at that, eating and drinking anything they find laying around, always trying to have a good time. And what it costs them is luck. You can't be a good-timer and still pay attention to your luck."

"That's true," agreed Cat. "I've seen plenty of Dogs, including some big, strong ones, done in because they lost their heads while good-timing." Cat reached into his inside coat pocket and found himself a seegar and lit it up. He took a puff, tilted up his head to blow out a cloud of smoke, and lifted his nose high in the air as if to smell the lovely odor of himself. "Cats," he said, pointing his seegar at Dog, "are so smart and serious they never lose their heads while good-timing."

"Cats are certainly smart and righteous," agreed Rat. Cat lifted his nose even higher and his smile stretched bigger. "Which," Rat continued, "is why so many of them are so stupid about luck."

Cat snapped his head back down, hunched up his shoulders, and glared a long, mean look at Rat. Rat began to feel mighty uncomfortable, and he wished he hadn't said the words 'Cat' and 'stupid' in the same breath.

"How's that again, Fat Rat?" yowled Cat. "You said something about Cats being stupid?"

"Now Cat," said Rat with a nervous twitch of his skin-tail, "the smartness of Cats is well-known. Every Rat will tell you that Cats are the smartest folks on four feet." Cat gave a little nod of his head and unsquinted his eyes some, and Rat relaxed some. "But whenever some kind of trouble starts to brewing, Cats believe, it seems to me, that knowing the right and wrong of the matter is more important than being on the lucky side of the outcome."

"How you talk, Rat!" said Dog, scratching his ear and searching his own coat pockets to see if he could find himself a make-a-point seegar, which of course he didn't have. "Why if folks live the way they want to live, that won't suit you at all."

"Hush, Dog!" yowled Cat. "We are talking about living and luck. You got no luck, except every day bad luck, because you never think ahead. As a matter of fact, you never think ahead, or backwards, or sideways, or any way at all. But that can't be the reason Cats occasionally meet up with bad luck, because a Cat never takes a careless or thoughtless step."

"So true," agreed Rat. "Cats are so smart that they know the right way to act every minute. But Cats lose their luck when they fail to separate the right way to act from the lucky way the act."

"There's 'a rat' in separate," said Dog. "I read that in a book once. It was a long time ago, but I'm sure that's what it said: 'separate' has 'a rat' in the middle of it."

"May we go on with this discussion now, Dog?" asked Cat with a little bow.

"Sure," said Dog.

"Please continue, Rat," said Cat.

"Now, Cats don't go stumbling into bad luck the way dogs do," said Rat, "but when bad luck comes chasing after them, Cats refuse to step out of the way. That's why you find plenty of big, strong Cats, and good fighters too – the kind of Cats that would never waste time fooling around like a Dog – still end up on the worst end of a back-alley scrap.

"When a Cat gets to feeling he's in the right, nothing is going to change his mind. No shoe, stick, rock, brick, poison, car, truck, bus or ugly kid. Nothing. And none of those things is going to bring you any luck. If you want good luck, you got to be willing to get out of the way of bad luck."

Cat rolled his eyes and wiped his nose on Dog's sleeve. "Well, Rat, that kind of talk just goes to show what a low animal a Rat is!" Rat could plainly see that Cat was in a huff. "A Rat will sit right here on his fat behind and snipe at Cats because they choose to do what's right. Don't you think a Cat knows the best way to get along in this world? A Cat wouldn't lower himself to act like a Rat for all the tea in China. No Cat is going to do anything that is not right and proper. That's the way it is: Cats must be Cats!"

"Now, now Cat," said Rat. "Don't be thinking I'm talking down the ways of Cats. They're fine ways. Perfect ways. For Cats. I'm just explaining about luck, and why Rats seem to have so much. The ways of Cats just ain't the lucky ways."

"Tell us, Rat," said Dog, "just what it is that you Rats do so much better than Dogs and Cats. You can tell us how wrong we act and how that brings us bad luck, but can you tell us how we should act to bring us some good luck?"

"I think you should act just the way you do act, Dog," said Rat. "And Cat, too. It ain't my plan to try and change your ways. You are going to stay Dog no matter what I say. And Cat will stay Cat. I am only explaining how a difference in the ways we live makes a difference in how much luck comes to us. Do you see, Dog?"

"I see, Rat," said Dog. "But I still want to know what exactly it is that you do that causes you to have so much luck."

Rat leaned way back and hooked his thumbs in his vest pockets, getting himself ready to deliver a lecture to Dog. "Above all, Dog, Rats are firm believers in getting on. We don't ask for much, and we're always willing to avoid trouble.

"Let me give you a few specifics about the way we live. Rats stay out of streets, preferring the quiet and safety of alleys, sewers, and dumps. Rats refuse to fool around; we just never do it, ever. Rats are easily frightened. They less we are seen, the more we like it. Furthermore, Rats never claim something that someone else might take away from us, and we never assume that being right means being unbreakable.

"And that," said Rat, "is what Rats call 'getting on.' And why we have so much of what you and Cat seem to think is good luck."

Rat stretched up on this tip-toes and fluffed his fur to warm himself. "Say, Cat," he said, "do you think the exhaust fan beneath this grate has shut off? There ain't much warm air coming out."

"Don't you worry about the fan, Rat," said Cat. "Just get on with your Rat-luck lecture and let the fan take care of itself."

Rat sat down with a hurt look on his wrinkly face. He wished he had never started talking about luck if it was going to make everyone so mean-mouthed.

"Well, Cat," continued Rat, "if you must hear it all, it is not luck that makes Rats what they are but just plain hard work. You got to work to stay out of the way of bad luck. Sure, Rats don't have Dogs' good times, and we often feel unhappy about that. And we don't have smartness or pride like Cats, and we often feel ashamed of that.

"But always and forever, we Rats get on. We get on from day to day, doing the best we can. We hide from kids, run at the first sight of a truck, never bad-mouth anyone, and never claim anything that can't be held in one paw. Rats get on. And that's all there is to Rat-luck."

Rat stood up and took a little bow to show that his lecture had come to an end. Then he sat back down and looked up his nose at Dog and Cat. Cat looked at Rat like he was something that smelled bad. Dog was shaking his head. It didn't make any sense to him.

"See here, Rat," said Dog. "If that's how it is with Rats, how come you got that bent and broken nose? Why is the tip of your skin-tail cut off? How is it that you are all scarred and puffy around the eyes? If you work so hard at getting on, why do you have such a beat-up look, Rat?"

Rat ran a knobby paw dawn the length of his bent nose and glanced at his poor tail. "Even when you do your best to just get on," Rat said to Dog, "the world takes its toll."

"Well, I'd rather be a Cat anytime," said Cat.

"And I'd rather be a Dog," said Dog.

"But I'm a Rat," said Rat.

Then they were all quiet and sat cold and trembling as the last of the warm air puffed out of the exhaust grate and drifted away and let the freezing night close in around them. A hard winter was coming fast. They could all feel it.

"W-walking might ch-chase the ch-chill out," chattered Dog.

"And maybe we could find another warm spot," said Rat.

So without too much grumbling they got themselves up and set off down the street. The morning sky was just turning pale as they started off together: Scrawny Dog, Hungry Cat, and Fat Rat.

Chapter 2
In The City

A few warm days followed the wintry cold spell, and for a while it seemed as though things were going to be all right. Since hot-air exhaust grates weren't needed on warm nights, Scrawny Dog, Hungry Cat and Fat Rat didn't see much of one another for several days.

Cat went back to his summer sleeping place in an old tire that had been thrown up onto a garage roof. Rat slept in his trash can bedroom, comfortable in the daily garbage that was as much fun to play with, and sometimes to eat, as it was to sleep on. "I'm the best dang thing in the can," he often said, which is a Rat kind of joke. Dog slept wherever he fell down at night.

But they all found themselves together again one cold, sunny morning, grubbing for food in the alley behind South Restaurant Street. And that was the day the bad news came.

Rat was examining the contents of a big green trash dumpster, digging through it with his front paws while his back paws clung to the handle on the outside. You could see his tail end, but not his head. Cat was smoking a crooked black seegar and holding up the lid of the dumpster while he waited for Rat to find something worth eating.

Dog came jogging down the alley with his ears not brushed. He saw all of Cat and half of Rat investigating the dumpster, and he bounced over to see what it was all about. He was ready for breakfast.

"If I had a dollar, I'd buy me a cup of coffee," Dog said to Cat.

"But you ain't got a dollar," answered Cat.

"Well, if I had I would," said Dog.

Rat straightened up to try and figure that one out and banged his head on an empty pickle jar. "Lag dag 'em, Dog!" he snapped as he rubbed his head. "That didn't make any sense."

"What didn't make sense?" asked Dog.

"That what you said about coffee and the dollar."

Dog gave him a funny look. "You must have heard wrong, Rat," he said. "I don't have a dollar."

"I know that," chided Rat. "But then you said 'if you had, you would,' and just what does 'would' mean? Coffee or dollar?"

"Rat," said Dog, "that don't make any sense."

"Dog," said Rat, "you are sometimes so stupid." Rat put his head and front paws back down into the trash dumpster.

"What's Rat so mean-mouthed about this morning?" Dog asked Cat.

"Maybe he doesn't like coffee," said Cat. "Or maybe because he can't find a thing for us to eat in this worthless dumpster."

"Hey, Rat!" hollered Dog. "It's no use looking in that green dumpster. The people at this restaurant eat everything. Believe me, I've tried it before."

"Well, which one should I try?" asked Rat, raising his head up above the edge.

"Do that one over there," said Cat, pointing at a greasy, red dumpster a long way down the alley.

Rat mumbled and grumbled as he tried to scramble backwards out the dumpster. He was hanging onto the edge and swinging back and forth, afraid to drop to the ground, when Cat decided to relight his seegar. When Cat reaching into his inside coat pocket to get his box of wooden matches, he let go of the dumpster lid that he had been holding up. It came down with a crash, right on the knobby toes of Rat's front paws.

Rat squealed and snatched his paws out from under the lid so fast that he lost his balance, fell off the dumpster, and belly-whomped onto a pink cardboard box on the ground. He lay there with his breath knocked out of hi m and moaned and wished his ribs didn't hurt so bad. Dog and Cat sat back and laughed until they howled.

Then, just as fast as a Weasel with his whiskers on fire, a red-eyed Mouse with a silver hat pin leaped out of the pink cardboard box and commenced to pull on Rat's tail!

"Get off of there, you house-breaker!" the Mouse yelled at poor old Rat. "Off or I'll pin ye!"

"Get him, baby Mouse!" shouted a shrill voice from inside the box.

"I'll get him, Ma!" yelled the Mouse.

Rat moaned.

"Hey there, Mouse," said Cat in his most serious voice, "don't you go needling our pal or we'll fix ya."

"Oh, yeah?" yelled the Mouse. "And just what do you think you're going to do?"

"If you give us any trouble, we'll scruff ya," said Cat.

"Oh, yeah?" said the Mouse, making a little Mouse-sneer with his face. "You think the likes of ye can scruff the likes of me, do ye? Do ye?!"

"You tell him, baby Mouse!" screamed the voice inside the box.

"I'll tell him, Ma!" said the Mouse. He grabbed the hat pin with both of his front paws and swung it in a circle over his head like it was a sword. "I'll pin all of ye!" he yelled.

"Pin 'em, baby Mouse!" screamed the voice from inside the box.

"I'll pin 'em, Ma!" yelled the Mouse.

Rat scurried off the top of the pink cardboard box, which was a bit crushed-down where he had belly-whomped onto it, and he limped over to sit down next to Cat and Dog. His ribs still hurt.

"Nyah! Nyah! Nyah!" yelled the Mouse as he jabbed the hat pin at each of them.

Cat handed his seegar to Dog, rolled up his sleeves, and spit on the knuckles of his right paw. "That's all we're taking from you, Mouse," he yowled. "Now I'm going to scruff ya!"

"Nyah!" screeched the Mouse, jabbing at Cat with his hat pin.

Cat snatched down and came up with a chunk of broken brick in his paw. Mouse looked at that chunk of brick for about one second flat, threw down his hat pin, and ran back into the pink cardboard box as fast as his short little mouse legs could run.

"Keep your bricks off my baby Mouse!" screamed the voice from inside the box.

"You tell him, Ma!" yelled the Mouse, hiding in a back corner of the box.

Cat tossed the chunk of brick over his shoulder. "A hat pin. A box Mouse with a danged hat pin," he said as he reached over and took his seegar back from Dog.

"Whew!" said Dog as he shook his ears and blinked smoke out of his eyes.

Rat just moaned again and felt his ribs, wondering if any of them were broken.

By now, the day was getting a bit too cold and their stomachs were just a bit too hungry for things to seem right. Rat was grumpy and told Dog and Cat that he would not search through another dumpster because his ribs and his front toes hurt. Cat wanted to finish smoking his seegar in peace. Dog wanted to run somewhere and find something to do. But first, all three of them wanted something to eat.

"Wish we had some fish," said Cat.

"Wish was had some soup," said Dog.

"Wish we had some cheese," said Rat.

"Want some peanuts?" asked Squirrel from the roof of the restaurant.

Dog looked up. "Hiya, Squirrel," he said.

"Hiya, Dog," said Squirrel. "Want some peanuts?"

"You got some peanuts?" asked Cat.

"Of course he has," Dog chided Cat.

"Maybe I have," said Squirrel. "What have you got to swap for them?"

"How about this busted watch?" asked Rat, pulling a big gold watch out of his vest pocket.

Squirrel spit. "Busted watch? You think I'm a Crow? Busted watch! That ain't worth nothing."

"Well, it ticks if you shake it," said Rat, who thought it was a fine watch.

"No," said Squirrel. "It's got to be something else."

"How about some marbles?" asked Dog.

"Nope," answered Squirrel. "What I really need is a shirt. A good, heavy, warm, wool shirt, because winter is coming."

Cat thought for a minute. "Okay," he said. "Rat, you give Squirrel your wool shirt."

"What!" squawked Rat. "Fooey to that! Why my shirt?"

"Because you always got at least three," explained Cat, "and me and Dog only got one each apiece."

"And don't I feel bad for you because I'm so shirt-rich," back-talk-ed Rat.

"Aw, come on, Rat," pleaded Dog. "We'll get you another shirt sometime. We haven't had any peanuts in a month. Maybe two months."

"My shirt for a bag of nuts," huffed Rat, but he took off his coat, and then his vest, and then his brown outside shirt, and finally his good, heavy, warm, wool inside shirt. Dog saw that Rat had another shirt under the wool one, with fewer holes and more pockets and even a nice clean collar.

Squirrel climbed down from the roof on the drain pipe with a big paper bag clutched in one front paw. Rat gave Squirrel his good wool shirt, and Squirrel folded it and stuffed it into the inside pocket of his jacket. He handed the bag of peanuts to Rat. "Your shirt – your nuts," he said.

"Thanks," said Rat, taking the paper bag.

Squirrel climbed halfway up the drain pipe, then stopped and came back down. "Hey," he asked Dog, Cat and Rat, "aren't you three being awful risky?"

"Nope," said Dog.

"What do you mean?" asked Cat.

"Haven't you heard the new rule?" asked Squirrel.

"What new rule?" asked Rat.

"NO ANIMALS ALLOWED IN THE CITY. That's the new rule," said Squirrel.

"What!" barked Dog.

"No animals are allowed in the City from now on," said Squirrel. "Least ways no free ones. Every animal running free is in big trouble."

"How come?" asked Dog.

"Because that's the new rule, that's how come," said Squirrel.

"But why?" asked Rat.

"Listen," said Squirrel, "when there's a rule there doesn't have to be any 'why' or 'how come.' It's a rule. That's all there is to it. So you better watch out is what. And why. And how come. You just better watch out."

"Okay, Squirrel, we will," said Rat.

Squirrel climbed back onto the restaurant roof, and the three of them sat down and looked at the bag of peanuts.

"I hope they do get ye!" screamed a Mouse voice from inside the pink cardboard box. "I hope they get all of ye!"

"Dang them box Mice," snarled Cat. "Let's move down the alley a ways.

"Let's go somewhere else," said Rat.

"Where we going to go?" asked Dog.

"We got to decide," said Cat.

"I know what we got to decide first," said Dog.

"What?" asked Rat.

"We got to decide if we're going to stick together."

They hunkered down in a little circle, facing one another, and they all sat quiet for a minute. Two minutes.

"I say we stick," started Rat.

"I'll stick," agreed Dog.

"It's stick then," said Cat. "Spit on it."

They all spit and slapped their front paws on the ground in the center of their circle.

"Okay now," said Rat, "together, what are we going to do? Are we staying in the City?"

"Either we stay, or we go," said Cat.

"The City's a pretty regular place in the winter," said Dog.

"But there's the new rule," said Rat.

"Rules schmules!" yowled Cat. "It's been our City for years, ain't it?"

"Maybe not anymore, though," replied Rat. "Maybe we should leave."

"Rules schmules!"

"If we leave the City, where would we go?" asked Dog. "We've never been no place but the City. I don't know any other place."

Rat thought for a minute. "I've heard there is a trash Dump up north of the City. Why don't we go take a look at it?"

"A Dump?" said Dog.

"Yes," said Rat. "In the country."

"They say the country is beautiful in the winter," said Dog.

"I don't like it," argued Cat. "Living in some dirty Dump in the freezing cold winter because of some new rule."

"Aw, come on, Cat," pleaded Rat. "Let's just go see it. If you don't like it, we'll come right back."

Cat muttered something under his breath. It sounded like "Rules schmules."

"Hey, I've got an idea!" yelped Dog. Cat and Rat stared at him. Dog didn't have very many ideas, so it took them by surprise.

"What's your idea?" Rat asked, real prodently.

"Let's eat the peanuts," said Dog.

"Just hold onto your tail for a minute, Dog," snipped Rat. Dog grabbed hold of his tail. "How about it, Cat?" asked Rat. "Do we go north into the country, just for a look?"

Cat spit out a little piece of seegar and made a sour face. "Okay, you skin-tail, we'll go," he said. "But if it ain't purr-fect for this Cat, we come right back. Understood?"

"Hoo-ray!" cheered Dog. "All settled. We're going to the Dump. Now open that bag of peanuts, Rat-face."

Rat hated to be called 'skin-tail' or 'Rat-face.' But seeing as things were going so smoothly right then, he didn't scold Dog or Cat, he just dumped out the peanuts in a big pile on the ground. They ate them all. They didn't leave a single one for the box Mice.

Chapter 3
At The Dump

"It's canned stuff for me," said Dog as they walked along the roadside, heading out of the City. They were keeping an eye out for a northbound truck so they could hitch a ride. "Canned stuff and no foolin'. Whether it's peas or pudding or pumpkin or potmeat or potatoes, it don't make no difference as long as it's in a can. Stuff always tastes better out of a can."

"That's how Dog got to be so shaggy-faced," snickered Rat. "Eating out of cans with sharp edges." That was a Rat-kind of joke. Cat and Dog did not think it was funny.

"Why, Dog would even eat doorknobs if he found them in a can," Rat continued. "Me, I don't eat nothing that I can't gnaw on, because if it can be gnawed you know two things about it: it's good for your teeth and it's got vitamins."

Cat sniffed. "A Rat will eat anything that will fit into his mouth," he said. "Gnawed stuff – huh! What folks should eat is stuff that's plain. No fancy-fixed vegetables, no bitter stuff – except for tea and coffee, of course – and nothing with sauce. Just plain stuff. Especially fresh-cut meat. The main thing about choosing stuff to eat is this: if it smells like it hasn't been fooled with too much, it's probably plain enough to eat."

"Look sharp!" barked Dog. "There's a truck stopping just ahead."

The three of them went barreling down the road as fast as they could run, which is not very fast for a Fat Rat, and they piled into the back of a canvas-topped orange truck. It started with a jerk and a lurch, and Cat and Rat had to grab hold of Dog to keep him from bouncing out of the back end.

"Oh, boy! This is really moving along," hollered Dog as he watched the telephone poles whiz by the truck with the zzwhipf sound they make when you are going really fast.

"I hope we don't zoom right by the trash Dump," whined Rat. "We can't jump out of the truck while we're going this fast."

"Yessir, worry-Rat, yessir," scolded Cat. Rat hated to be called 'worry-Rat,' but he didn't give Cat any back-talk about it. "You go ahead and freeze us all to death, Rat, by letting all the cold wind in the whole world blow under that canvas top you're holding up to keep a lookout. Then when we are all turned into lumps of fur and ice, it won't matter how fast this truck is going when it comes time to jump off at the Dump."

"Well, I don't want us to go zooming right by it," back-talked Rat.

"Just sit yourself back, Rat," Cat said, "and let old Cat's smart-mind do all the thinking and figuring. When we get close to the Dump, old Cat's smart-mind will know."

Rat threw down the corner of the truck's canvas top with his feelings hurt. "Well, old Cat's smart-mind is going to be singing a sad song when we miss the jump-off place at the Dump because of old Cat's cold-tail," he chided.

Cat waved his paw under Rat's nose and stretched back to relax. "Old Cat's smart-mind sees all and knows all," he said. "When we get near the Dump, I'll get us ready to jump off this truck. Then we'll go find us some grub." Cat closed his eyes and took a long draw on his seegar to show Rat what a wonderful sense of know-where-I-am his smart-mind had.

"Get us ready to jump!?" yelped Dog. "Jump from a fast-moving truck? Cheese-rinds to that, Cat! No jumping. Not this Puppydog. We are going to wait for this truck to stop, and then we are going to climb out like folks with good sense. Jump? Hah! Cheese-rinds!"

"But what if this truck doesn't stop at the Dump, Dog?" asked Rat.

"Cheese-rinds!"

"But…"

"Cheese-rinds! Cheese-rinds! Cheese-cheese-cheese-rinds," said Dog. "Nobody with a lick of good sense would jump from a moving truck."

Rat twitched his tail and looked at Cat. Cat still had his eyes closed and acted as though he had not heard a word Dog said. Rat thought maybe Cat was taking a nap. He raised the corner of the canvas top ever so slightly, peeked outside, and smelled the wind. "Say, Cat," he said, "I think I can smell the…"

""Dump!" yelled Cat, jumping to his feet. "We are at the Dump and it's time to jump." He scrambled onto the truck's tailgate, pushing Dog and Rat ahead of him. "Everybody out!"

Rat looked at the rock-filled roadside ditch and the fence posts and telephone poles flashing by, and he moaned his little Ratty moan. "This doesn't seem like a good idea, Cat," he whined.

"Go on, jump!" shouted Cat. "This was all your idea, not mine."

"Ohhhhh!" moaned Rat. "Well, here's for bread crusts and pie!" He grabbed his nose in both front paws and stepped off the tailgate. Wham! Slam! Whomp! Rat landed in the ditch and dust went flying everywhere.

"None of that for me!" howled Dog as he stepped back from the edge of the tail gate and tried to get back inside the truck.

Cat grabbed Dog by the sleeve, pointed at the sky and yelled, "Hey, Dog, look at those green Ducks!"

"Where?" asked Dog, stepping to the edge of the tailgate and looking up.

"Out and away!" shouted Cat, and he gave Dog a good hard boot to the left of his tail that sent him flying off the truck.

"HEEEE! HOOOO!" Dog grabbed his long curly ears and covered his eyes. Then – WHUMP!! — he landed hard and flat on his back in a soft pile of dirt and went sliding and skidding about nineteen and a half feet along the bottom of the ditch.

Cat laughed so hard that he slipped off the edge of the tailgate and did a flip-flop through the air. He almost caught his balance and landed on his feet – the way Cats usually do – but he was twisted sideways, so he stumbled and fell. One roll and one bounce and he came up clean, still laughing.

"Ho ho ho ho hee ho!" Cat yowled, holding onto his sides to keep from splitting his vest. "Did you see that old Dog hit the ditch? Ha ha ha ha hooo! Some fun, huh? Some laughs! Did you see it, Rat?"

Rat came limping along just as Dog was unwinding his ears from around his head. "Ohhh! Ohh, nooo. Ohhh!" Dog was whining. "I never landed like that before. Never. No. Not ever. I'm a gone Dog, Rat. Cat threw me off the truck and slammed me down on my middle back at a hundred miles per hour. I guess it's done me for good. I'm a goner. So long, Rat. Good-bye forever."

"You don't look all that hurt to me, Dog," Rat said to him after a close doctorlook and a few pokes and prods that made Dog yip. "You landed on a part of the ditch where it's soft."

"Sure, that's fine for you to say," whined Dog. "You wanted to jump. This was all your bright idea. Besides, it ain't your middle back that is all broken and smashed to pieces. So it's all just fine for you."

"And I say it's just fine for you too, Dog," said Cat, "because it is." Cat wiped the last of the laugh-tears from his eyes. Then he sniffed a sniff. And another sniff. "Say, Rat," he said. "Do you smell bird poo?" He sniffed again and wrinkled his face. "Whew!"

Rat leaned his head forward and sniffed. "I sure do, Cat," he said. "Strong, too. Really smelly bird poo. It's awful." He held his nose.

Cat shook his head and took a step back. "What a stink!" he said. I wonder where it's from?"

"It's probably from birds," said Dog, trying to sit up and holding onto his aching middle back. "That's where bird poo is usually from."

"Very amusing," sniffed Cat. "But where is it here-abouts. It's got to be close, and I don't want to step in it." Cat took another look at Dog. "Why, Dog, it's… No. Yes. Yessir! The bird poo is on Dog. Look, it's on your pants, Dog. There is a big smear of bird poo right there on Dog's pants." Cat shook his head in a no-use-for-that sort of way. "My that is ugly, Dog."

"Well, if that ain't the beans," moaned Dog as he looked down at his pants. "See here, Cat, what you've done with your kicking me around? And it ain't like that kind of bird poo is going to wash right out either."

"Oh, hush up, Dog," said Rat, who was pretty beat-up himself and had his clothes all covered with dirt from tumbling through the ditch. "We can clean that out later with some vinegar and a scrub brush. We got more important things to do right now. First off, we got to find the Dump."

"Find the Dump?" said Cat. "Why, didn't I tell you that my smart-mind knows right where it is?"

"Okay, so where is it, Cat's smart-mind?" asked Rat.

"It's right over there," Cat said, pointing to no place in particular.

"Where?" asked Rat.

"Oh, right around here somewhere," said Cat, turning around in a circle and looking everywhere. "Let me see…"

"If the wind was blowing from the right direction, we could smell it," said Rat.

"I smell great," said Dog, tapping his nose.

"Oh no you don't" said Cat. "You smell like stinky bird poo."

"Just smell, will you, Dog?" chided Rat.

Dog stuck his nose high in the air and took a big snort. "It's way up the road, probably about a mile," he said.

Rat gave Cat a real sour look, but Cat acted like he was searching in his pockets for a box of matches and didn't notice. "Cat's smart-mind," sassed Rat. He looked down the road and saw a big green metal sign on wooden posts. It said: County Landfill Entrance – 1 Mile

"You were right, Dog," said Rat. "The Dump is a whole mile away."

"It is?" said Dog."

"Yes," said Rat. "That's what it says on the sign."

"That sign?" asked Dog pointing down the road.

"Yes, that sign," said Rat. "Can't you read?"

"Oh, sure I can read," said Dog. "Just not signs."

"Well, let's start walking," said Cat. "Unless you want to hitch a ride on another truck."

"No!" said Dog. "No more trucks."

"Now let's all be prodent," warned Rat. "Let's be careful when we get there."

"What a worry-Rat," said Cat. He knew Rat hated to be called a worry-Rat. "All we got to do is walk right in and start looking for some eats. There aren't any rules like NO ANIMALS ALLOWED

IN THE DUMP, are there?"

"I just don't want to be brick-batted by some kid who hasn't got anything better to do than hang around a Dump all day," said Rat. "I had an uncle who was killed that way."

"Just look at these pants," said Dog.

Finally, after a long, slow walk, they came to the gates of the trash Dump. It was a good Dump, as far as eatables go, especially since Dog, Cat and Rat arrived just after the morning deliveries. Dog cut his lip on the sharp edge of a can of vanilla pudding, and Cat couldn't find enough fresh-cut meat, but before long they were all stuffed and satisfied and sitting in the sunshine on top of a piano box in garbage pit number four. The sun was warming their cold toes, and it was beginning to be a real good day.

"Maybe we should set up here for keeps," said Dog, blinking his sleepy eyes. "If we're looking for a regular meals kind of place, this looks like one of those places that often are."

"Often are what?" asked Rat.

"Regular," answered Dog. He yawned a big yawn.

"Dog that doesn't make any sense," said Rat. He shook his head. Sometimes it was hard for him to understand what Dog was talking about. So he quit trying. He stood up on his tiptoes on top of the piano box and looked around as far as he could see.

"From what I can see of it from here, it doesn't look bad," he said. "But we ought to check everything about it before we decide."

Cat took a draw on his seegar. "This is no place to spend a winter," he said.

"What's wrong with it?" asked Dog.

"Look up, Dog," said Cat with a little sigh. Dog looked up. "What do you see?" asked Cat?

"A blue sky with seven Redwing Blackbirds flying over us and a cloud that looks like a big white bunny, and…"

"Dog," said Cat in his you-make-me-tired voice.

"What?"

"I like to have a roof between me and the sky in the winter," said Cat. "If you two want to shiver your ears off living in some freezing cold Dump that's fine with old Cat, but I'm going to live someplace warm and cozy, not here."

"Why, we could live right here in this piano box," said Dog.

"Pianos," said Cat, "live in piano boxes, not Cats."

"Let's look around for a better place to stay," said Rat.

"Before supper?" asked Dog.

Cat grabbed Dog by the tail and pulled him off the top of the piano box. Rat hopped off too, and they started walking up the side of the garbage pit.

"We know there's nothing on that side," said Cat, waving a paw behind them," so let's try this side. You never know what you might find."

"Probably a mean kid with a stick or a rock," whined Rat. "We better be careful."

"Will you stop worrying?" scolded Cat. "If we were all as careful as you we'd never do anything."

"Well, just remember," snipped Rat, "when something terrible happens, I told you that something terrible was probably going to happen."

They reached the top edge of the pit, and Dog looked over. "Hey!" he barked. "There's a house."

Cat looked and gave a whistle. "Now that's a real house," he said.

Rat was too short to see over the edge of the pit. "Let me see! Let me see!" he said, jumping up and down and tugging at Dog's tail. Then he poked Cat in the ribs. "I want to see it. Pick me up so I can see it."

Cat and Dog picked him up so he could look over the top edge of the pit and see the house. Rat's eyes got big as baseballs. "That is some house," he said.

There are little houses, medium houses, big houses, and really big houses, but this house was the biggest of the really big houses. Cat and Dog and Rat together didn't have enough toes to count all the windows. The roof had seven peaks and seven chimneys. A porch covered the whole front, and round tower stood in one corner. It was dark and empty, and it looked kind of scary, but like Rat said, it was some house.

"It has three stories," said Rat. "It's a Three-Story House."

"Let's go have a look," said Cat.

Good idea," said Dog, and they dropped Rat.

Fat Rat slid all the way down the side of garbage pit number four on his round tummy, and a big tin can that came tumbling after him conked him right on his head. He moaned. Then he sat up and rubbed his head. "See that, you old funnies?" he yelled at Dog and Cat. "You see me catch that can right in the head? That was because you went and dropped me."

"Too bad it didn't knock you lummy," said Cat. "Then maybe you'd be quiet and stop complaining all the time." He and Dog climbed over the top edge of the pit and started off toward the big house. Rat had to scramble to catch up.

Chapter 4
The Three-Story House

Dog, Cat, and Rat sat in the grass by the front porch and looked up at Three-Story House. From this close it didn't seem so scary, just empty.

"Should we knock?" asked Dog.

"Who would answer?" said Cat. "Let's just bust a window and go in."

"Maybe we should find a hole," suggested Rat.

"We could spend half the day looking for a hole that's not there,

Rat," said Cat. "And even if we found one, it would probably be big enough for a Rat but not for Dog or me."

"Why don't we just open the door?" asked Dog. He wiped his front paws on his pants, jumped onto the big front porch, and walked right up to the front door.

"Sure! That's right! Great idea," hollered Rat. "Just open the door and get yourself shot!"

Cat jumped onto the porch with Dog. Together they pushed on the big blue front door, and it swung open with a squeak. "Well, it's open," said Cat. "Let's go in." He held the door so Dog could go in first.

"Sure! That's great. Both of you get yourselves shot!" Rat hollered again.

Dog walked in, and Cat waited to see what Dog would find inside. "It's empty," yelled Dog. His voice echoed in the big front room of the house. Cat snuffed out his seegar, put it into his vest pocket, and walked in.

Rat moaned and whined and fiddled with his tail. Finally he crawled up on the porch, stuck his nose a little way through the doorway, and then followed Dog and Cat into the house. He walked into a big high-ceilinged room with doors and windows everywhere. There was a huge brick fireplace built into one wall and a gold chandelier hung from the center of the ceiling. Cat and Dog were nowhere to be seen. Rat scurried across the room and looked through a doorway. It opened into the tower with a spiral staircase going up the center.

"Cat went up those stairs," said Dog as he pushed a big brown stuffed easy chair into the front room. Rat jumped about three and a half feet in the air, Dog scared him so bad. He landed on his back and put his hand over his heart. "I'm a dead Rat," he moaned. "You have done scared me to my death, Dog."

Dog shook his head. "You should try to relax, Rat." he said. "Being as nervous as you never did nobody no good." He ran out of the living room through a door on the far side, and Rat could see that door led into a kitchen. Rat wanted to say some smart back-talk to Dog, but he couldn't think of anything before Dog was out of the room, so he yelled after him, "Oh, yeah?" Then Rat sat down in a corner of the front room and waited for his heartbeat to slow and his nervous mind to calm down. He decided to wait for Cat before he did any exploring.

When Cat came down out of the tower, Rat was sitting and fidgeting in the corner of the front room and Dog was sitting in his brown easy chair drinking a bottle of blueberry soda. His mouth was purple all the way out to his whiskers because he was a sloppy drinker.

"Hey," said Cat, "is that blueberry soda?"

"It certainly tastes so," replied Dog.

"Where did you get it?" asked Cat.

"From the cupboard over the kitchen sink," said Dog. "There's lots of it. Forty-three bottles, I think."

"You can't count to forty-three, Dog," chided Rat. Dog just shrugged his shoulders and took another swallow of his blueberry soda. Cat's mouth began to water.

"Is it cold, Dog?" asked Cat.

"Kinda cold," said Dog smacking his lips. He pressed his left front paw against the side of the soda bottle. "Yeah, kinda cold."

"Was it in the ice box?" asked Rat.

"You stupid Rat," sassed Cat. "Dog just told us it was in the cupboard over the sink, so it wasn't in the ice box."

"That's right," said Dog. "In the cupboard, not in the ice box."

"Then how come it's cold?" asked Rat.

"I ran some cold tap water over the bottle for a couple minutes," explained Dog as he wiped a drip of purple soda off his mouth with his sleeve.

"Cold tap water!" snapped Cat. "Let me feel that soda bottle, Dog." He jumped up onto the brown easy chair and put his paw on the bottle. "That soda ain't cold, Dog," he said. "That soda is warm."

Dog felt the bottle again. "Yeah," he agreed, "it's kinda warm."

"Warm blueberry soda," said Rat. "My, that is awful, Dog."

"No, it's good," said Dog. "It tastes like blueberry pie."

"Yessir," said Cat. "Good old sugary, watery, purple, warm, blueberry pie."

"Yep. And there's lots of it, too," said Dog. "How lucky is that?"

"Well, unless you can find some way to make it cold, it's all yours, Dog," said Rat.

"Okay," said Dog. He took another swallow, which was about the last one in the bottle.

"Come on, Rat," said Cat. "Let's go find the cellar."

"Shouldn't we explore the rest of the house first and find the cellar last?" asked Rat.

"I already explored the whole rest of the house," said Cat. "It has nineteen rooms, five on this floor and seven each on the second and third floors. And every room has tall windows and is painted different colors. It's got six stairways and seven fireplaces and a great big kitchen, and an attic full of furniture and old treasure chests and books and pictures. It's even got a couple hidden closets. The only thing left to find is the cellar, so get up off your furry fat behind and let's go find it."

"We'll be right back," Rat said to Dog, who was sticking his tongue down into the soda bottle.

"Dun fugit abow suther," mumbled Dog.

"What?" asked Rat.

Dog took his tongue out of the bottle. "I said, don't forget about supper."

"Come on will you, Rat," scolded Cat from outside the doorway, and Rat ran after him.

The cellar doors were just outside the kitchen entrance at the back of the house. They were big, heavy steel double doors, the kind that are usually found in castles and forts. Cat was unfastening the latch to the doors when Rat came running out of the kitchen and almost bumped into him.

"Watch it, Rat!" snapped Cat. "You want me to pinch myself?"

"No," answered Rat, although he thought it might be just fine if Cat pinched himself.

"Well then, run more carefully." Cat gave one cellar door a good pull, and it opened part way. "Get yourself under the door there, Rat, and give it a push," Cat said. Rat didn't like that idea, but he squeezed himself under the edge of the door and pushed while Cat pulled. The door opened farther, and Cat and Rat heard some skittering noises down in the cellar.

"Hold the door open while I look down in there, Rat," said Cat. Rat braced his back paws on the door frame, stood up, and held the door open with his front legs stretched up over his head as far as they could reach. Cat let go of the handle, and door was almost too heavy for Rat to hold up by himself. Cat searched around and found a long stick and used it to prop open the door. "Okay, Rat, you can let her go," he said. Rat let go of the door and jumped back. The door stayed open and Rat sat down on the top step of the stairway that went down into the cellar. Cat lit a seegar, took a puff, and sat beside Rat.

Rat hunched forward and looked down the stairs. "My, it is dark down there, Cat," he said.

""Yeah, real dark," agreed Cat, blowing out a big cloud of seegar smoke and scratching his head. "Did you hear that scritching and scratching noise down there?" he asked.

"Yes," said Rat. "I wonder what it is. It doesn't sound very big."

Cat looked at him like he was the most stupid animal in the whole world. "Oh, it doesn't sound very big?" he chided. "And how big, Rat, does bad business have to sound?"

"Well, bigger than that, anyway," said Rat. He listened close, but the scritching and scratching noises had stopped. "Do you know what I think, Cat?" he said. "I think maybe we should close this door and forget that there is a cellar under this house. Who needs a cellar anyway?"

Cat chomped down on his seegar. "No, we got to find out what's what," he said. He rolled up his sleeves, made a fist, and spit on his knuckles. "I'll brace the door while you go down there and have a look around."

"Me!" yiped Rat. "For sure not. That's what I got to say. If you want to know what's what, you can go down there and look for yourself."

"Oh, Rat," soothed Cat, "the noise doesn't sound very big."

"Just how big does bad business have to sound?" Rat sassed back. "Me, Rat, says NO, Cat, and that's that."

"Now listen, Rat," said Cat, "let's figure this out for a minute. If we're going to live in this house we better know everything about it before we move in, or there could be real trouble. Right?"

"Maybe," whined Rat.

"Right," said Cat. "So we have to check this cellar, and we might as well do it the best way we can. Right?"

"I don't know," hedged Rat.

"Right," said Cat. "And the best way is for me to do the brace-the-door part and you do the go-down-and-look-in-the-cellar part because you ain't tall enough or strong enough to brace the door once you're on the stairs."

"If I don't go on the stairs I'll be tall enough," said Rat.

"Rat, we have to go down the stairs to look into the cellar," explained Cat.

"We!" said Rat. "You mean both of us are going down the stairs?"

"Why of course," assured Cat. "I'm going to go just as far down the stairs as I can go and still be able to brace the door open."

"How far am I going down?" asked Rat.

"Only far enough to see what that noise is," said Cat patting Rat on the back and helping him onto his feet. "Now, let me brace that door and let's get started."

Rat watched Cat lean on paw against the door, but he didn't start down the stairs. He felt his feet must be stuck in mud or something, because they wouldn't move. "I don't know about this Cat," he moaned. "What if it grabs me?"

"Then I'll come running down the steps and prang it a good one on its head," said Cat. "Don't you worry about that, Rat."

"Oh, this will come to no good," whined Rat. "I just know this will come to no good." He hopped down onto the top step and bent way over to peer into the gloomy cellar. He couldn't see anything.

"Go on down, Rat," said Cat. "Bracing this door open ain't exactly a fun time."

So Rat started to take another step, and he cupped his front paws around his mouth and shouted, "Okay down there whatever you are, you better not have any trouble in mind, because I might be coming down, and… and… and my friend the Cat…"

And when Rat said 'Cat' all sorts of squealing and shrieking and running and bumping noises came up the stairs from the dark cellar. Rat jumped back to the top of the stairs so fast he nearly knocked down Cat.

"Now look what we've done," moaned Rat, grabbing his tail and jerking it around like a snagged rope.

"Why, that ain't nothing but noise," yowled Cat. "Noise never did nothin' to nobody. Which is why it's safe for you to go down and look and see what it is, because it's just noise."

"Then you go down there and look for yourself," said Rat with a big wave of his paw. He shouldn't have waved it though, because his tail was still in it, and he pulled his feet right out from under himself.

He landed with a bump on the very edge of the top step. "Help me, Cat!" he screamed. "It's going to get me!"

Cat looked down on the top step, and there was Rat – scared stiff. Then Cat turned his head to listen, and there was that cellar noise – scary noise. And he figured that since Rat was already scared, and since he wasn't scared yet, and whoever went down into that cellar was going to be scared, and there wasn't any good reason for both of them to be scared, that Rat might was well be the one who went down. So when Rat tried to stand up, Cat used his foot – now he never kicked Rat, even Rat would say that Cat never kicked him – he just used his foot to help Rat down the stairs.

Rat bounced on every stair (there were eleven of them) and landed with a WHUMP! down in the pitch dark on the cellar floor. All the noise stopped.

"AAAHHCAT!!"

"It was the most awful scream that Cat had ever heard. It was the Rat. He sounded as though he was half-ready to be pranged on the head and half-ready to prang somebody on the head. Cat took the seegar out of his mouth. "Everything all right down there, Rat?" he called down the stairs.

There were some dusting-myself-off noises in the dark of the cellar. "Cat," said Rat in an echoing voice.

"Yeah?" answered Cat.

"Cat, do you remember how you traded my shirt to the Squirrel, Cat?"

"Yeah."

"And Cat, do you remember how you kicked Dog off the tailgate of the truck, Cat?"

"Yeah."

And Cat, do you remember how you dropped me down the side of the garbage pit, Cat?"

"Yeah."

"Well, Cat," said Rat with a little sigh and some more dusting-off sounds, "this is the worst. The very worst."

Cat thought for a minute. "Why don't you come back up the stairs, Rat?"

"No" said Rat. "No, I'm going to sit here in the dark and let the noises get me."

"Noises don't get you, Rat," said Cat. "Things get you."

"Well then, I'm going to sit here in the dark and let the things get me," whined Rat.

Cat bent down, grabbed the handle of the other half of the cellar door and pulled it wide open. More light shone down the stairs but the cellar was still dark. "Cat stepped down onto the top stair. "Come on back up, Rat. I didn't mean to push you down the stairs."

"Oh yes you did!" said Rat.

"Well, I wish I didn't mean to. Come on up."

"No," said Rat. "The noise is going to get me, and it's all your fault."

"Rat, if you don't come up out of there, I'm going to come down," warned Cat.

Rat didn't say anything, but Cat heard him give another sad little sigh.

"Do you hear me, Rat?" yelled Cat.

Rat probably did hear him, but he still didn't say anything.

"I will, Rat. I'll come down there," said Cat.

Rat didn't answer.

Cat muttered and mumbled and then snuffed out his seegar and put it in his vest pocket. He started down the stairs, into the dark, holding one paw ahead of him so that he wouldn't bump into anything. He went slowly, one step at a time. It was so dark at the bottom that he couldn't see a thing. He stood still and waited until his eyes adjusted, then he looked down and saw that he was standing on something round. It was Rat's tail.

"I'm sorry, Rat," said Cat, high-stepping off of it.

"It doesn't matter," said Rat. He was sitting on the bottom stair with his face in his paws.

"Now don't be that way, Rat," said Cat. I won't do it again."

"Oh no, that's fine," sobbed Rat with a big, drippy tear running down his bent nose. "Just push me down the stairs, backwards, in the dark, where the noises can get me, and then say 'don't be that way.' That's just fine."

"Oh, Rat," said Cat, sitting beside him on the bottom step and putting his arm around Rat's shoulders. "I promise not to dirty-Cat-trick you again. Honest." He reached into his pocket. "Here. Have a seegar."

"No sir, no sir," mumbled Rat as he took the seegar. "I'm going to be a smarter Rat from now on. Smarter. Smarr-tter. Do you hear me, Cat?"

"Sure, sure, Rat. Of course you will," said Cat as he handed Rat one of his own clean handkerchiefs to wipe his teary-wet nose. Then Cat stood up. "Well, we're down here, Rat, so we might as well have a look around." Rat moaned.

Chapter 5
Lady Mouse And Others

"Look at this cellar, Rat," said Cat. "Why there's all kinds of stuff down here. Look at these bedsprings." Cat climbed up onto one of the twenty-six junk piles in the cellar and sat on the rusty bedsprings at the top. He started bouncing like a wild-Cat.

Rat watched him for a while. A big smile started to grow on Cat's face as he bounced higher and higher. He had a dreamy look in his eyes like he didn't know anything but bedsprings. Finally, Rat couldn't stand to be left out of the fun. He jumped off the bottom stair and ran to the foot of the junk pile. He put his paw on the edge of the bedsprings and felt them going up and down, up and down, and heard their metally squeak.

"Hey, I'm going to jump on there with you, Cat!" said Rat with the little laugh. Each time the springs went up Rat got himself ready to jump, but each time the springs came down he couldn't make his legs do it.

"Hop on, Fat Rat!" yelled Cat with a big come-on wave of his paw. Rat muttered and mumbled because Car was such a show-off to ride the springs with only one paw holding on. Rat wound himself up once more to make the jump, and even though his legs still wouldn't do it, he flew into the air as Cat grabbed him by the scruff of the neck and pulled him on.

"Gawk!" hollered Rat. He landed on his fat stomach right across the bounciest part of the bedsprings. Cat was going like sixty, and with Rat on the corner the springs were bouncing and twisting every which way you can point.

"Whoa! Now whoa! Whoa now!" yelled Rat. His tail was getting pinched each time they came down, and each time they went up he was so busy holding on that he forgot to pull it out of the way.

"Ha ha!" laughed Cat. "Watch this, Rat! I'm going to stand up!" Cat hopped onto his feet and tried hard to keep his balance, but he fell right on top of Rat and the bedsprings began to slide.

""Whoa! Whoa!" yelled Rat. They tumbled down the side of the junk pile and knocked over a lamp.

"Whoa! Whoa-ho-ho!" yelled Cat. They spilled onto the floor, and boxes and bags full of junk went flying in all directions. Rat ended up under the bedsprings with his head stuck in a round cardboard box, and Cat was almost completely buried under a stack of newspapers. Cat was laughing like a Woodpecker on a bee tree. Rat had his paws covering his eyes so he wouldn't have to look at his hurt tail.

"WHAT do you two think you're doing!?" screeched someone from a back corner of the cellar.

"Don't let it get me, Cat!" screamed Rat as he pulled the box tighter over his head.

"Just WHO do you think you are?" the voice screamed again.

Cat was untangling himself from the pile of newspapers, which put him in a sour mood, and he didn't like for anybody to tell him how to behave even when he was in a good mood. "Just WHO do you think YOU are?" he snapped right back.

"I live down here in this cellar," said the voice, "and I will have to fix all the things you are breaking!" The voice moved out of the dark corner, and Cat saw it was a Mouse.

"Why, this ain't nothin' but junk," yowled Cat. "Who cares if it gets broken?"

"Well, it may be junk to you," said the Mouse, "but it is my home and you are tearing it to pieces."

Rat lifted the edge of the box on his head and peeked out and saw the Mouse. "Are you another one of those box Mice?" he asked.

"No, I am not a box Mouse. I am a cellar Mouse, though I wouldn't have much of a cellar if you had your way."

Cat couldn't think of anything smart and sassy to reply, so he thumbed his nose at the Mouse and said, "Ahhh – pajamas!"

"Don't you talk that way to me!" scolded the Mouse lifting her chin and stamping her foot. "I am a Lady Mouse, and I won't stand for it."

"Well," said Cat, "I am a Cat, and I'll stand you on your head."

"Tsk-tsk, Cat," tsked Rat. "You can't talk that way to a lady."

"Why not?" asked Cat.

"It just isn't done."

"Ahh – pajamas!"

Lady Mouse marched across the cellar, reached under the bed-springs, flipped the box off Rat's head, and grabbed him by the ear. "You come out from under there and clean up this mess, and I mean right now, mister."

Rat scrambled out and picked up the broken lamp.

"Don't you do it, Rat!" yowled Cat.

Rat dropped the lamp.

"You pick up that lamp," Lady Mouse told him.

Rat picked up the lamp.

"Listen, Mouse," said Cat, "this is our house, and we don't have to do anything we don't want to do. Understand? Put down that lamp, Rat."

Rat dropped the lamp.

"If you think for one minute that this house belongs to you, you have another think coming," said Lady Mouse. "You better go talk to Skunk and Weasel and the Rabbits and Chipmunk and Crow and Bluebird and Owl and goodness knows how many others, because we ALL live here, and this is OUR house. Now pick up that lamp!"

Rat picked up the lamp.

"Drop that lamp, Rat," said Cat. "Now you listen here, Mouse. I don't know any of those other folks, but if you think that they – or you – can tell me and my pals that we can't live in this Three Story House we found to live in, well I'm going to give you a second chance to think different." Cat wasn't sure exactly what he said, but he knew exactly what he meant.

"Pick up that lamp, you smelly Rat," said Lady Mouse in a huff. "Now, I don't know what kind of Cat you think you are…"

"The finest sort," sassed Cat. "Drop that lamp, Rat."

"Pick up that lamp! We had better go see the rest of the folks who live in this house and then you will find out just how much claim you have to it, you common alley-Cat," said Lady Mouse. "And I can assure you that they will not take this matter lightly."

"That's fine with me," snarled Cat. Let's go see them right now. Every one of them. Put down that lamp, Rat, and let's get going."

"Good heavens yes!" Lady Mouse snipped at Rat. "What are you doing holding that piece of junk anyway, you stupid Rat?" She went stamping up the cellar stairs with Cat right behind her. He was puffing hard on his seegar and trying to make it stink. Rat tagged along after them.

They paraded into the kitchen, and Lady Mouse swung open the door to the broom closet. "Here is Skunk," she said.

Cat looked into the broom closet. "Where?" he asked.

Lady Mouse peeked around the door and looked all over the closet, even up on the top shelf. "Well, he's usually here," she said in an angry voice. "I'm sure he won't be gone long. We can come back later."

"I don't think a Skunk really lives here," said Cat.

Lady Mouse whirled around to face Cat and put her front paws on her hips. "Are you calling me a liar?" she asked.

"I ain't the one showing me an empty closet," sassed Cat.

Lady Mouse slammed the door and marched into the front room. Dog was asleep in the brown chair.

"Get up, you mongrel," said Lady Mouse, tapping Dog on his nose. "You're sleeping in Chipmunk's chair."

Dog opened one eye. He was sleepy and had no idea what was going on or who this Mouse was. He yawned and stretched all four legs. "What?" he asked Lady Mouse.

"That's Chipmunk's chair," she said.

"I ain't no Chipmunk," said Dog, a little insulted.

"But I am," said a squeaky voice from somewhere inside the stuffing of the chair. A brown-striped head popped out of the cushion and looked around. "Is that you, Lady Mouse?" the Chipmunk asked. "Is is okay to come out?"

"Yes, Chipmunk, you can come out," said Lady Mouse. "And would you please tell these three rude animals who this house belongs to."

Chipmunk thought for a moment. "I don't know who it belongs to," he said.

"It belongs to us," said Cat.

"That has not yet been determined," Lady Mouse said to Cat. "Chipmunk, would you call everyone to meet together in the front room so that we can settle this matter once and for all and send these three ruffians on their way?"

"Okay," said Chipmunk. "But Skunk and the Otters and the Rabbits aren't here. They went out for lunch in the garden."

"Never you mind," said Lady Mouse. "As long as you can find Crow and a few others, we will get along nicely."

Chipmunk climbed out of the chair, walked through the tower doorway, and started up the spiral staircase. "I didn't know this house belonged to anybody," he said. "Nobody ever tells me anything."

Lady Mouse looked at Dog and fluffed up her ears. "I'm sorry I called you a mongrel," she said. "I was a bit upset."

"Oh, that's alright," said Dog. "I've been called worse. Have a drink of blueberry soda?" He held out a sticky bottle.

Lady Mouse gasped and turned pale around the eyes. Lady Mice do not drink from bottles. Except maybe this one time, since Dog seemed so nice. "Why, thank you," she said, and she took a little sip.

Chipmunk came down the stairs followed by five odd birds: a feathery Bluebird, an Owl, a Thrush, an English Sparrow, and a Crow. The Bluebird was first in line, and she gabbed and chattered all the way across the room.

"What difference does it make who the house belongs to?" she tweeted. "Nobody ever cared about it before. Why does Lady Mouse bring these sorts of animals into the house anyway? And Crow, why did you make us all hide when they got here? We should have figured this all out in the beginning, the very beginning. No one ever does any planning around here."

"Who is that bird?" Dog asked Chipmunk.

"Have you ever heard of the Bluebird of Happiness?" asked Chipmunk.

"Why, yes I have," said Dog.

"Well, this is not her," said Chipmunk. "This is her sister, the Bluebird of Daffyness. She's kind of a featherhead."

Crow was at the end of the line of odd birds. He hopped over to Lady Mouse, straightened his black silk frock coat, and tipped his stovepipe top hat. "How are you this afternoon, Lady Mouse," he croaked. "I understand there is a little problem of some sort which requires my professional services and advice."

"Who is this character?" asked Cat.

"Call me Crow," said the bird. "The house attorney at caw, advisor, counselor, juris prunes, and know-it-all. Every sort of legal opinion and advice, all for the asking, and a small retainer fee and commission, of course."

"He's a common scavenger Crow," Chipmunk whispered to Cat, "but he's the only one we've got."

"I don't know if I trust this bird," Cat said.

"Shush!" Lady Mouse scolded Cat. "Would you please let me explain the situation to him?"

"There's a 'sit' in 'situation'," said Dog. "I read that in a book once."

"I would love to hear about it sometime," said Lady Mouse, batting her eyes at Dog. "But right now we need to straighten out this business with the help and advice of Crow."

"Go right ahead," said Dog. "I'm going to get me another bottle of blueberry soda." He walked off toward the kitchen.

"Now see here, Crow," said Lady Mouse, "this rude Cat and miserable Rat claim that the house belongs to them, and of course their friend that handsome and well-mannered Dog. I would like you to tell them who the rightful owners of this house are, and then order the Cat and the Rat to leave the premises immediately."

"Ah, yes. The rightful owners of this Three-Story House," said Crow, taking his eyeglasses from the inside pocket of his coat and balancing them on his beak. "I can't remember anyone ever mentioning it before, but I'm sure I have a signed and notarized document here to refresh my memory." He took a big binder of yellow papers from an outside pocket and began to look them over. "Yes, yes, yes. Here we have it," he said. "Statement of ownership... party of the first part... party of the second part... parties of several other parts... in agreement with... on specified date... with the full consent of... by the authority vested in me… complete and binding… habeas corpulent… ex post factoid… en loco parents. Yes! That's our answer. Plain as the writing on the wall."

"What is our answer?" asked Lady Mouse, her head spinning from Crow's law caws.

"In strict legal terms, no one has ever mentioned ownership before," explained Crow. "No animal who lives here has ever said that the Three-Story House was his, or hers, or theirs, or whomever's. I have a signed statement to that effect from every resident of the household."

"Skunk can't read or write," said Chipmunk.

"Neither can the Rabbits, Weasel, nor any of the featherhead birds," said Crow. "That is why I had to write it, read it aloud to myself, and sign it for each of them."

"Is that fair?" asked Lady Mouse.

"Ah, yes. Quite fair," said Crow. "None of them ever said I couldn't do it."

"Oh my," said Lady Mouse. "What does that mean? Who owns the house?"

"As far as legal aspects go and the courts would be concerned, this Three-Story House belongs to the Cat and his friends the Rat and the Dog, since they were the first to say that it is theirs. The three of them probably own it in equal shares, although they may have to engage my services to determine the exact percentages."

"Oh my goodness," said Lady Mouse, turning pale around the eyes again.

"Perhaps something could be arranged to alter the circumstances so that title of ownership and rights of residence would be interpreted more in your favor," Crow said to Lady Mouse. He turned to speak to Cat. "Sir, do you know how to read and write?"

"Yeah," said Cat. "I can read and write real good. And I know how to spell 'trouble for Crows,' too."

"Ah," said Crow. "Well then, Lady Mouse, I fear that it is beyond my powers to pursue any further action at this time." He turned to leave, then came back. "By the way, Mister Cat, if you would like me to serve eviction notices on all these other folks, you can find me in my office on the third floor from nine to five, Monday through Friday. Good day, Lady Mouse. I will send you a bill for services rendered, payment expected on the first of next month." Crow took off his glasses, hopped into the tower, and went up the spiral staircase.

"Now what's going to become of us?" squawked Bluebird. "We'll be thrown out in the cold, and it's all because of Lady Mouse being such a busy-body."

"Oh, my" said Lady Mouse, weaving and wavering. "I must sit down."

Dog had come back from the kitchen carrying a full bottle of blueberry soda. He put his arm around Lady Mouse and set her up in the big brown easy chair. "Don't you worry," he told her. "We're not going to make anyone leave this house. Are we Cat?"

Cat leaned against the fireplace and lit a fresh seegar. "How should I know?" he snapped. "I don't even know everyone yet."

"They're all nice," said Bluebird. "You'll like them."

"How many?" asked Cat.

"How many what?" replied Bluebird, a bit confused.

"How many animals live here?" said Cat.

"Well, let's see. There's me and the rest of the third floor birds…"

"The what?" asked Cat.

"The third floor birds. You have already met Crow, and you have seen Fool Owl and Thrush and one of the English."

"The English?"

"Sparrows," said Bluebird. "There are nine of them, I believe, always talking in that phony London accent, although I don't think a single one of them has ever been to England. They can be so annoying, but at least they're not Scots."

"Nine English Sparrows," said Cat.

"Yes," said Bluebird, "and two Pigeons, a Red-Headed Woodpecker, a Yellow-Shafted Flicker, and four Meadowlarks, who are most excellent singers I might add. Oh, also one Loon."

"Good grief!" said Cat, rubbing his paw across his face.

"Not, not a Grebe, a Loon," said Bluebird. "You can tell them apart because a Grebe does not have webbed feet."

"Twenty-two third floor birds," said Cat.

"More or less," said Bluebird.

"Then there's the second-floor animals," said Chipmunk.

"How many?" asked Cat.

"About twelve," said Chipmunk, counting on his toes. "There's the Otters…"

"The Otters?" asked Cat.

"He-Otter and She-Otter," said Chipmunk. "Quite a pair."

Who else?"

"Weasel, Raccoon, Frog…"

"Where does he live?" asked Cat.

"Bathtub," said Chipmunk. "And of course there's the back bedroom Rabbits. Five or six of them, I think, although it's hard to keep track of rabbits."

"On the first floor, Skunk lives in the kitchen broom closet," said Bluebird. "He's the house cook, and he makes the kitchen smell so bad that no one else can live there."

"Skunk stink?" asked Dog.

"Oregano and garlic and basil and rosemary and burnt peanut oil," said Bluebird. "He's not the best cook in the world."

"And in the cellar are the Mice," said Chipmunk.

"Lots of Mice?" asked Cat.

"Lady Mouse and four other junk Mice," said Bluebird.

"I am not a junk Mouse," huffed Lady Mouse.

"Well my dear, if you share your cellar with junk Mice, you must expect to be considered a junk Mouse," replied Bluebird with her beak in the air.

Cat puffed on his seegar and did some serious thinking. "Nobody lives in this first floor front room?" he asked.

"Chipmunk does," said Lady Mouse. "He lives in the brown easy chair."

"Well, me and Dog and Rat live here now," said Cat. "Rat can sleep in the corner, Dog in front of the fireplace, and I'm taking the easy chair."

"Hey!" barked Dog. "I had the easy chair."

"You don't know how to use it right," said Cat.

"What about me?" squeaked Chipmunk. "I live in the easy chair."

"You're moving upstairs," said Cat.

"Upstairs?"

"Yep. You can choose your floor."

Chipmunk bounced over to the easy chair, hopping mad, and took his extra shirt and two pair of socks from under the cushion. "Well, I'm not moving in with a bunch of feather-headed birds!" he whined to Cat. "I'm going to the second floor. Maybe Weasel will let me live in his closet." He started up the spiral staircase like it was a mile high and he was three days tired.

"That takes care of that," said Cat. "Nobody gets thrown out as long as everybody acts right and stays out of my way."

"There's just one thing left to do," said Dog.

"What's that?" asked Rat.

"Have a party," said Dog. "A big party. A house-warming party. We'll invite everybody and have blueberry soda and popcorn."

"We've never had a party before," said Lady Mouse.

"I'll teach you how to do one," said Dog. "We'll have it tonight. Tell everybody."

"Just tell the quiet folks," said Cat. "No rowdies."

"And you are specially invited, Lady Mouse," said Dog.

"Oh, my," said Lady Mouse.

Chapter 6
The Wassel Party

The evening turned chilly as the sun went down. Cat and Rat built a roaring fire in the fireplace and sat themselves down in front of it to warm their noses and toes.

"I guess the party will start pretty soon," said Rat.

"I reckon so," said Cat.

"Have you ever been to a party?" asked Rat.

"No," said Cat. "Have you?"

"No," said Rat. He tugged at a sore whisker. "I wonder what you do at a party."

"I don't know," said Cat.

"Dog must have been to lots of parties before," said Rat. "So he should know what to do."

"We'll know before too long," said Cat. "Here come the first party folks."

Bluebird was leading the third floor birds down the stairs. They were all dressed for a party and had their feathers fluffed and brushed. Crow had on his black frock coat and stovepipe hat, but he was also wearing a green tie and yellow spats. Fool Owl had on a pink shirt with lace collar and cuffs. Bluebird had curled her tail feathers and wore a necklace with blue glass beads and silver bells. Woodpecker was dressed in a black-barred tuxedo and had a long cigarette holder clamped in his beak, although he didn't have any cigarettes.

Thrush was wearing high black boots and had a matching black glove under one wing. The English Sparrows were all wearing brown cardigan sweaters and saying things to each other like "Oh I should say" and "Dashing, simply dashing." The Pigeons wore matching hula skirts and straw hats. Flicker was wearing his usual yellow vest and red bow tie, and the Meadowlarks were wearing bowler hats and were dressed like a barbershop quartet. Loon was wearing an orange rain slicker and had tried to put orange lipstick on her beak; it looked really bad.

"Dog told us to dress fancy," Bluebird said to Cat and Rat. "Do we look fancy?"

"I'll say you do," said Rat.

"You have to dress like that for a party?" asked Cat.

"I don't know," said Bluebird. "I've never been to a party before."

Next came the second floor animals. Dog must not have told them to dress fancy because they looked more or less regular, except that He-Otter and She-Otter were wearing matching red shirts that had the words "And I love you, too!" embroidered over their hearts. They liked to nuzzle and kiss all the time.

Weasel, Raccoon and Frog had on swimming suits. "Dog told us there could be a water fight," Raccoon told Cat.

"No water fights in the house," said Cat. "Ever."

"The Rabbits will come down later," said Weasel. "They're planning something special."

Chipmunk was sitting on the arm of his old easy chair. Lady Mouse and the other four junk Mice came up from the cellar and crept into the front room so quietly that no one noticed they were there until one of them tapped Rat on the shoulder and said, "I'm hungry. Is there going to be a dinner?"

"Partyfood! Partyfood!" yelled someone in the kitchen. There was a clang-clang on a brass cymbal, and through the kitchen door and into the front room came Skunk, dressed in a pink apron and pulling a rubber-wheeled wagon full of boxes, bottles, bags and cans. "I'm in charge of partyfood, because Dog said so, and I'm going to fix some delicious grub for everyone."

He took a wooden spoon from the wagon and hit the cymbal hard. Clang! "When you hear that sound," said Skunk, "it means that partyfood is ready and you should come to the kitchen and eat it." He put the cymbal and the spoon back into the wagon and pushed it back through the kitchen door. "Partyfood, coming up!"

Fool Owl tapped Rat on the shoulder. "You must understand that he is really a good character, just a bit boisterous," Owl said.

"What's boisterous?" asked Rat.

"Noisy. He's noisy," said Fool Owl.

"Who?"

"Skunk. But he's really a good fellow. I thought you should know," said Owl. "And now I must bid you adieu." He bowed low and then hopped off to tell someone else about Skunk and boisterous.

Rat sat down beside Cat who was searching in his pockets for a box of matches. He finally found it, but before he could light his seegar more and more folks were gabbing and talking and hooting and hollering in the front room.

Closest to Cat were Weasel and Chipmunk. Weasel was quiet most of the time, but he was always reaching into his shirt pocket for a green bottle of tongue drops. He sipped the drops from a hole in the bottle cap and said they made his mouth taste better and made his tongue feel wetter. Cat thought it was silly to worry so much about your tongue, but watching Weasel worry so much about his all the time made Cat start to worry about his own. It wasn't long before Cat was wishing that Weasel was somewhere else.

Chipmunk was hanging onto Weasel's sleeve and asking everyone a hundred questions every minute. Nobody can answer that many questions, but everyone was trying. Chipmunk had everyone talking at once, and no one could understand what anyone was saying. So he got upset and grabbed Weasel and walked off in a huff because no one was listening to him

He-Otter and She-Otter went off by themselves and sat next to the fire and didn't do any kind of partying. All they did was sit close to each other and talk quietly. Every once in a while She-Otter would sniff a soft little sniff and would not talk to He-Otter until he mumbled that he was sorry. Then she would give him a kiss on the cheek. Cat didn't know what it was all about, but it didn't seem to him to be any way to act.

When the Rabbits came bouncing into the front room it looked as if they would steal the show. They were all dressed in clown costumes and had their faces painted white, and if they weren't running and tumbling they were throwing each other's handkerchiefs into the fire or standing on each other's shoulders until the top Rabbit on the stack could touch the ceiling with his ears. Cat thought this was too much of a good thing, and he told Rat so. Rat shrugged his shoulders to show Cat that he didn't know what could be done about it.

While the Rabbits were running crazy the junk Mice huddled in a corner near Cat and Rat. One of them kept asking Cat for matches until Cat had given away his last one and had to relight his seegar from the burning log in the fireplace. As he puffed away he could see that all the folks were getting rowdy. Too rowdy.

Finally and at last, Dog pranced into the front room wearing a top hat and cape. It was his party, and he wanted everyone to know it. He tossed back his cape, took off his hat, reached deep inside it, and brought out a giant firecracker. With a little toss of his wrist, he threw it into the blazing fireplace. Cat grabbed Rat, pulled him behind the big brown chair, and threw himself down on the floor.

The firecracker went off with a BOOM! and a ROAR! Sparks, ashes, cinders and smoke blasted across the room, and the stack of Rabbits was blown to the four corners. A grey cloud of ashes and dust slowly rose to the ceiling, and nineteen folks lay on the floor with their fingers jammed in their ears and their eyes squinched tight. Dog was the only one left standing, and he looked a bit shaky.

"A thirty-two cent Big Bomber!" said Dog as he searched for his top hat. "Just about all the cash money I had, but nothing is too good for this party. I've been saving it for a week."

Cat sat up with his ears ringing and his eyes burning and he thought the worst was certainly over. He figured Dog couldn't top that firecracker trick and probably wouldn't even try. But he was wrong. Dog was just getting started with party tricks.

Before Rat's ears stopped whistling and buzzing, the Rabbits and Chipmunk and all the third floor birds were gathered around Dog, slapping him on the back, shaking his paw, and telling him what a fine way it was to start a party. Cat was still lying behind the brown chair looking at his smashed seegar. A Rabbit ran by and stepped on his tail. That was the clincher for Cat.

"Now, I enjoy a good time myself, Rat," he said, "but this party has just begun and it is already out of hand. I told everybody 'no rowdi-ness,' and I meant 'no rowdiness!' This is going to stop."

"What are you going to do?" asked Rat.

"I'm going to throw everybody out of this house," snarled Cat.

Rat thought for a second. "Why don't we talk to Dog about it?

Maybe he will quiet things down, and you won't have to stop the party." Cat nodded, and Rat scurried off to bring Dog around for a little talking-to.

"Have you got another one, Dog?" asked Chipmunk. "Another Big Bomber? It would be swell to do another one."

"Hoo-ray!" cheered the Rabbits. "Do it, Dog! Do another!"

Dog held up his paw to quiet the crowd. "Everything at the proper time, folks," he said. "This is a house-warming party, not the Fireworks of July."

"Oh, Dog…" said Rat, tugging at his cape.

"Just a minute there, Rat-face," said Dog, pulling his cape away. "I got to get things going."

"But, Dog…" said Rat.

"Tsk-tsk-tsk, Rat," said Dog, curling his tail. "You are going to spoil my grand entrance."

Rat could see that Dog was not to be talked to sensibly, so he did the only thing he could: he grabbed him by one shaggy ear and dragged him howling and yelping across the room to Cat who was puffing hard on his seegar by the fireplace and blowing clouds of smoke. When Rat let go of Dog's ear, Dog took a look at Cat's seegar-smoky face and thought it was on fire.

"FIRE! Fire on the Cat!" Dog yelled in his loudest voice.

"Hush up, Dog!" snapped Cat. Dog hushed up. "Now Dog," lectured Cat, "a party is one thing, but what is going on here is something else. Do you smell that firecracker smoke? Do you see all this dust and ashes coming down? Do you hear those noisy Rabbits? Do you see this tail?" Cat held up his tail, and Dog looked at the footprint on it.

"Why someone has stepped on your tail, Cat," said Dog, pointing at the dirty footprint. "Look-it, someone has stepped on your tail."

"I know that, you curly-eared Dog," yowled Cat. "That's what I'm talking about. This rowdiness has got to stop!"

But just at that moment, the Rabbits came running from the kitchen into the front room, and they were carrying a two-gallon metal bucket that sloshed water. "Where's the FI-YER?" hollered the biggest Rabbit. "We heard somebody yell, 'FI-YER'! Get that water bucket ready, Rabbits!"

"Oh, wet trouble," moaned Rat.

"No, there ain't no fire," yowled Cat.

"I thought the Cat was on fire," Dog tried to explain to the Rabbits.

"The Cat's on FI-YER!" shouted one of the Rabbits.

"Cat's on FI-YER!" shouted the rest of the Rabbits. They raised the bucket and threw two gallons of cold water at Cat. Cat ducked and the two gallons of cold water flew over his head. Rat ducked and the two gallons of cold water splashed down on top of him. The Rabbits all cheered and threw the empty bucket into the corner.

Dog looked down at Cat, who was dry but was mad as a wet hen. Then Dog looked at Rat, who was soaking wet and wringing water out of his pants. "Well," Dog announced to everyone in the room, "I guess it's time to make wassel."

"What's wassel?" asked Cat.

"Wassel is what you drink at a party," said Dog. "It is usually the best thing about a party. You dry off the Rat while I get some folks busy making the wassel in the bucket."

Cat looked at Rat, who was now wringing water out of his coat. "Are you dry, Rat?" asked Cat.

"Sure," whined Rat. "I get two hundred gallons of water thrown on me, and the next minute I'm dry. That's how it works. Someone gets soaked by two hundred gallons of water, and then in one minute he's dry."

"Quit your whining," scolded Cat. "Stand over there by the fireplace where it's warm and give me your shirt so I can wring it out for you."

"Sure," said Rat. "Stand me over by the fireplace. That will make everything better. That will make me dry."

"Will you stop moaning, Rat?" said Cat. "All you can do is whine and moan and whine and moan when there's supposed to be a party going on." Cat pushed Rat toward the fireplace, set up the empty bucket, and commenced to wring water out of Rat's shirt into it.

"Hey, don't do that!" Chipmunk said to Cat as he came out of the kitchen. "We got to make the wassel in that bucket."

"You make wassel in a two-gallon tin bucket?" asked Cat.

"Of course," said Chipmunk.

"How do you make it?" asked Cat.

"I don't know," said Chipmunk. "I never made wassel before. Dog just told me, 'Pour this bottle of juice into the bucket and set it over the fire.'" Chipmunk held up a big bottle of thick yellow juice, unscrewed the cap, and poured it into the bucket. "Move out of the way, Rat. I got to set this bucket over the fire."

"Sure," whined Rat. "I'll stand over here away from the warm fire, in a cold draft, and probably catch pneumonia and influenza so you can use the fireplace to cook that bucket full of yellow poison." Rat was not having much fun at this party, and he wanted everyone to know it.

Lady Mouse came into the room carrying a No. 10 tin can that was bigger than her. "Who's making the wassel?" she asked.

"We are," said Chipmunk, tapping the side of the bucket with a spoon.

"Dog says to pour this into it," said Lady Mouse.

"What is it?" asked Cat.

"I don't know," said Lady Mouse. "Dog found it at the Dump. When we opened it, it smelled kind of like peaches. Or maybe plums."

"Great," whined Rat. "More poison."

"These apple slices are supposed to go into the wassel bucket," said Weasel, dragging a box of apples across the room. "Dog told me so."

"Okay," said Chipmunk. "Toss them in."

"Great," said Rat. "Rotten apples."

Two Rabbits came through the kitchen door carrying a heavy crockery jug. Something green splashed out of the narrow top every time they hopped. "Dog says…"

"…to pour it into the wassel bucket," finished Chipmunk. "Go ahead."

Cat watched as the Rabbits poured the green liquid into the bucket with a glug, glug, glug sound. "Do you know that that is?" he asked.

"It's half blueberry soda," said one of the Rabbits. "The other half is something powdery that Skunk mixed with water from green paper packages."

"Water doesn't come in green paper packages," said Rat.

"The water wasn't in the green paper packages," scolded the Rabbit. "The powdery stuff was in the green paper packages. And Skunk mixed it with water from the faucet in the kitchen sink."

"Oh," said Rat who was a little embarrassed.

Finally, Dog came back into the front room pulling Skunk's partyfood wagon behind him. Skunk was pushing. A three-quart clear glass bottle was in the wagon, and Dog had a one-pound box of ground cinnamon in his coat pocket. "Hold it right there, Skunk," said Dog. He took the box out of his pocket, ripped off the top, and poured the whole pound of cinnamon into the bucket. He smiled at Cat. "I like the wassel to be real cinnamony," Dog said. "That way it tastes good all night."

He threw the empty box into the fire and jumped into the wagon. "And now for the juice-de-gras," he said. Dog unscrewed the cap and tipped the bottle over the bucket. The juice bloop-bloop-blooped out of the bottle and sizzled as it ran down the side of the hot bucket.

"That's enough, Dog," said Skunk.

"It's never enough when some is left in the bottle," said Dog. He kept pouring until the last drop plinked into the full bucket. Then he grabbed the spoon from Chipmunk and started stirring slow and steady.

"Now this is real wassel!" barked Dog.

"How can you tell?" asked Chipmunk.

"When the apples turn brown and melt, that's real wassel," explained Dog.

Everyone was standing around the fireplace smelling the cinnamon-and-apple odor of the wassel. Even though it also smelled a little like turpentine, Rat wished he had some to drink. Cat edged up to the bucket and tried to put his paw into it to get a little taste. Dog cracked him on the knuckles with the spoon.

"Drink but don't touch," said Dog. "It's not good for your fur to touch it."

Cat gave him a mean look. "We then, give me some," he snarled.

"Okay, I guess it's ready," said Dog. "Everybody get themselves a can or a cup."

Cat grabbed two tin cans that were lying on the floor while everyone else scrambled into the kitchen to find their own. "Here, Rat," he said, handing him one of the cans. "Let's you and me give it a try."

Dog dipped a canful for each of them, and then dipped one for himself. Rat took a little sip and smacked his lips. "Good," he said. "It's good."

"Of course it is," said Dog. "It's wassel. Wassel is always good." He took a big gulp from his can and sloshed it around in his mouth. "Just right on the cinnamon," he said.

Cat watched Rat and Dog for a minute. They seemed okay. He sniffed his can of wassel and then took a sip. It was hot and sweet and sour and cinnamony in his mouth. He swallowed, and it made him feel warm inside. "Yep, it's good," he said. He drank down the rest and handed his can back to Dog. "Dip me another one," he said.

Dog was busy dipping cans for everyone, but he wasn't too busy to dip his own can the most. Dog and Cat and Rat drank a lot of wassel. Everyone drank a lot of wassel. Everyone kept drinking wassel until the wassel was gone.

Now the thing about wassel is this: It makes your tummy warm and it tastes good, but it makes your head dizzy and it makes some folks act funny. So it was not long before Cat and Rat forgot all about ending the party or stopping the rowdiness or making folks act properly. Rat didn't care that he was all wet, and Cat had stepped on his own tail.

"What we need here…" said Cat.

"…yes, indeed…" said Rat.

"… is a box of matches to light this seegar." Cat held his seegar in front of Rat's nose and pointed at it. "This seegar, right here."

"I bet they got a box of matches upstairs," said Dog.

"Who does?" asked Cat.

"The Rabbits."

"What are they doing upstairs?"

"Having a snowball fight," said Dog.

"But there is no snow upstairs," argued Rat.

"No, but there are lots of pillows in Weasel's room," explained Dog. "He collects them. Weasel collects pillows. Feather pillows. Lots of them."

Weasel sat up from where he was sleeping on the floor. "Hey, wait!" he yelled.

"Wait what?" asked Cat.

"How come the Rabbits didn't ask me?"

"To use your pillows?"

"No, to snowball fight."

"Well, then, come with me, Weasel," said Cat, getting to his feet and giving a swish of the cape he had taken from Dog. "Let's go hunt Rabbits!" Cat and Weasel walked off toward the stairway, arm in arm, singing some French song that Rat did not care to know.

"I'm glad I'm not up there," said Bluebird, who was sitting on the floor beside Rat.

"Why?" asked Rat.

"It's dark up there."

"So what?"

"Well," said Bluebird, fluffing up, "I'm kind of soft and feathery – like a pillow."

"Oh, yes," said Rat, nodding his head. "Oh, yes, I see. Yes, those Rabbits might very well mistake you for a pillow in the dark. Toss you around."

"Yes, exactly" said Bluebird as she went to sleep.

"Yes, exactly," repeated Rat.

Bluebird began to snore softly. She didn't wake up even when Skunk hit his cymbal – CLANG! CLANG! CLANG! – to announce that partyfood was ready to eat. Well, thought Rat, I should go to the kitchen and get a bite to gnaw on. He looked around as he walked through the kitchen door, and standing around the table were Crow and Lady Mouse and the junk Mice and He-Otter and She-Otter. Skunk was standing on top of the table. He was wearing a chef's hat and had a big ladle in his paw.

"We're making hot stewballs," Skunk said to Rat. "Want to help?"

"Nope," said Rat. "I want something to eat."

"Hot stewballs are something to eat, you stupid Rat," chided Lady Mouse.

"Not for me," answered Rat. "I want something I can gnaw on." He pulled open a cupboard door and took out a bag of Dog's radishes. Then he filled a glass jar with water from the faucet in the sink. He carried it all back into the front room and sat on the floor by the brown chair. He ate two radishes and took a big drink of water from the glass jar. He was glad everything was quiet, and he thought he might go to sleep himself.

Just as he was nodding off, Cat came stumbling down the spiral staircase and sat beside him. Cat stuck a bent and broken seegar in his mouth and smoothed his ruffled left ear with one paw. "Rat, it is getting out of hand upstairs," Cat said as he felt around for where he had put his tail. "That thing isn't under a rocking chair is it, Rat?"

"Here," said Rat, as he handed Cat his tail.

Cat thanked Rat with a nod of his head and put the tip of his tail under his back right paw for safekeeping. Rat bit another chunk out of a radish.

"Where'd you get them?" asked Cat as he stuck his seegar in his eye and then in his mouth.

"They're Dog's," answered Rat with a munchy crunch.

"Dog's radishes, huh? Where'd you get them?"

"Kitchen."

"Well, I don't want any radishes. No sir, no radishes for me," said Cat, trying to strike a match on the floor rug to light his seegar. The match wouldn't light. He tried it five more times, then decided he didn't have to actually light the seegar to smoke it; they always last longer cold and don't taste much different. He looked at the match. "Would you put this match in your coat pocket and save it for me Rat?"

"Sure," said Rat, reaching for the match.

Cat snatched it back. "Will you give it to me when I ask for it later?"

"Sure." Rat put the match in his inside coat pocket as Cat watched him carefully.

"If those are Dog's radishes, why are you eating them?"

"Hungry," munch-mumbled Rat. He leaned over to get a drink of water from the glass jar and accidentally dropped half a radish into it. Plunk. It floated on the water just out of Rat's reach. He wrapped both his front legs around the jar, pulled it into his lap, and squeezed his face down into the mouth of the jar to grab the radish in his teeth. SLOOMP! His whole head went into the jar, and he grabbed the radish. But he couldn't pull his head back out. He started bubbling. Cat heard the bubbling and looked over and saw Rat's head in the jar. It looked odd.

"Hwealbp!" bubbled Rat.

Cat jumped up. "What are you doing in there, Rat?" he asked.

"Durwhundin!!" bubbled Rat.

Cat grabbed the bottom of the jar and tilted it up to try to pull it off Rat's head. All the water slopped out in blubs and gurgles. Rat was all wet again, sitting in a puddle with a jar over his head. Cat tugged a time or two, but he couldn't get the jar off, so he scooted Rat into the corner and leaned the jar back against the two walls. That made Rat look straight up at the ceiling through the bottom of the jar. The radish was still in his mouth.

"Thanths," Rat said to Cat.

Cat reached into Rat's inside coat pocket to get his match, but it was all wet. He put the cold seegar back in his mouth and chewed on it. "We got to get your head out of there, Rat."

"Yemp," agreed Rat.

Cat sat down to think. The inside of the glass jar was so steamed up from Rat's breathing that his head could hardly be seen. Fool Owl came strolling along and tried to peer through the glass, then he tapped it with the walking stick he was carrying under his wing. "Whoo's in there?" he whooed.

"Ihms meh, Rhat," answered Rat. He couldn't talk clearly because of the radish being in his mouth and his whole head being in the jar. His voice sounded like an echo.

Owl stared at the jar for a minute and blinked his eyes slowly.

"Ravished for a radish, eh? Well that's certainly Rattish. Tsk-tsk-tsk." Owl tapped the jar with his stick with each tsk. "If I were you, I'd give him his walking papers, Cat."

"You'd what?" asked Cat.

"Give him his walking papers and send him on his way," said Owl. "Can't keep a clear head. No outlook. No foresight. We can't have that. Give him his papers and send him on." Owl took a bit of tissue paper from his vest pocket and stuffed it into the cuff of his shirt sleeve. "So much for that jarring conundrum," he said with a deep bow. "Good night, Monsignor Cat."

Cat chomped on his seegar as Fool Owl walked away. "We'll find a way to get you out of there, Rat." Rat didn't answer but Cat heard him gnawing on the radish. "You wait here while I get Dog and see what we can do about this." He splashed out of the corner and walked toward the spiral staircase, but before he could start up Dog came running down with a tuft of feathers stuck in one ear. Cat grabbed him by the coat sleeve before he could dash by, and Dog ran three circles around him and then tripped and fell on his tail.

"Hiya, Cat!" he barked. "Some stuff, huh? Some party, huh?"

Cat gave Dog a shake. "Listen, Dog! Rat has stuck his head in a jar, and we got to do something about it."

Dog scratched his head. "Huh?" he said.

"Come over here," said Cat. "He grabbed Dog by the ear and led him to the corner where Rat was propped up with his head in the glass jar. Dog took one look and the fur on his back stood on end.

"What is that?' he whispered to Cat.

"That's Rat."

Dog shuddered. "What happened to his head?"

"He got it stuck in that jar," yowled Cat. "Now what are we going to do about it?"

"Let me see," answered Dog. He walked over to take a look at Rat, but by now the inside of the jar was steamed up solid and he couldn't see inside. "You in there, Rat?" hollered Dog.

"You don't have to yell," echoed Rat. "I can hear, you know." He sounded terrible with his head in a jar.

"Maybe you can see him through the bottom of the jar," Cat said to Dog.

"Let's turn it down and take a look," said Dog. They each took a side of the jar and lowered it down until Rat's face could be seen through the bottom. Dog put his nose up close and peered in. There was old Fat Rat. The bottom of the glass jar had letters on it, so Rat's face seemed to be split into seven parts. He had one big eye the shape of an S, and a little Y-shaped ear. His whiskers looked like a cobweb. Rat saw Dog looking in at him and tried to give him a big smile, but with the funny-bottomed jar and the pieces of radish in his mouth, he turned into something that was all teeth.

"Dang!" barked Dog and dropped the jar. It hit the floor with a clunk.

"Oooww!" yelled Rat.

"Hey, watch it, Dog," scolded Cat. "You could give him a permanent hum in his head."

"Sorry," said Dog. "Maybe we should set him back up." He and Cat hefted the jar and leaned it back into the corner. "Now what'll we do?"

"Got a match?" asked Cat. Dog searched in his pockets and found a match. Cat lit his seegar, which was soggy by now. He blew out a cloud of smoke and thought for a minute. "I guess we could try tugging, prying, twisting or breaking," he said.

"Ought we to ask Rat which he would prefer?" suggested Dog.

"I don't see much use in that, Dog," said Cat. "Rat probably wouldn't like any of those ideas and would just waste our time with his whining."

"Yeah," agreed Dog. "He's just that way, ain't he?" He whapped his tail on the floor two or three times while he rolled up his sleeves.

"Well, let's start the action!"

"Hold on, hold on," Cat said, waving his fuming seegar under Dog's nose. "We better get some help. This looks like a hard job."

"I'll get the Rabbits!" barked Dog.

"No!" yowled Cat. "We need help from folks who won't ruin Rat's head. You get Skunk and I'll get Chipmunk."

"How about He-Otter?" asked Dog.

"Okay, but no rowdies."

Dog went running to the kitchen while Cat looked for Chipmunk in the front room. The kitchen was full of people drinking wassel, and up on the table was Skunk, fixing hot stewballs. Lady Mouse was sitting in Skunk's partyfood wagon with boxes of spices all around her, and every time he yelled "pepper" or "bay leaves" or some other spice, she would stand in the wagon and hand it to him.

Dog put one foot on the edge of the wagon and yelled, "Hey, Skunk!"

"What?" asked Skunk, looking over the side of the table.

"Come to the front room and help us get Rat's head out of a jar."

"Wait one minute, Dog," said Skunk. "Hand me that chili powder, Lady Mouse." She hopped up and searched through the wagon until she found a red box marked "Chili Powder," then stood on her tip-toes and handed it to Skunk.

"Hurry, will you, Skunk," yelped Dog.

"Hold your pants on, Dog," said Skunk. Dog hitched up his pants. Skunk held a hot stewball in his left paw and took the box of chili powder from Lady Mouse. He flipped open the lid with his nose and let fly two giant boomer sneezes. He shook lots of powder out of the box. Some of it hit the hot stewball, but most of it went down the front of his pants and into his shoes.

Skunk held up the finished hot stewball and looked at it with pride. "Another one done and ready!" he said. "Who wants it?" No one said anything. Skunk looked all around the kitchen for some-one who might eat that hot stewball. "Done and ready!" he called again. "Who wants it?" No one wanted it, so Skunk shrugged his shoulders and tossed it onto the pile of thirteen hot stewballs on the table. Skunk saw Dog eying the pile. "Every one of them a succulent morsel, too," said Skunk.

He handed the box of chili powder down to Lady Mouse and dusted off his neck and shoulders. "Now, what is the problem, Dog?"

"Rat's got his head stuck in a jar," said Dog, "and he wants it pulled off." The whole kitchen got real quiet.

"Why would he want his head pulled off?" asked Lady Mouse in a quivery voice.

"He don't want his head pulled off," said Dog, putting a paw over one eye. "He wants the jar pulled off."

"Dog means that Rat wants to have the jar pulled off, not have his head pulled off," chirped Bluebird. "The jar, Lady Mouse, not his head."

"Come and help us will you, Skunk?" pleaded Dog. "Rat doesn't want to spend the whole rest of the night with a jar on his head."

"That's exactly right, Skunk," chattered Bluebird. "Rat does not want to have a jar on his head all night, Skunk. He wants that jar pulled off his head, Skunk."

"And hurry," said Dog as he ran through the doorway to the front room. Skunk jumped off the kitchen table and followed. Everyone headed for the front room. They all wanted to see whether Rat got the jar or his head pulled off.

Cat and Chipmunk were sitting on the floor debating the matter of the jar and the Rat. Chipmunk was waving his paw under Cat's nose and bobbing his head up and down as he talked fast.

"I say what goes in comes out in similar fashion but backwards," said Chipmunk. "If we butter the neck and keep the ears pressed down, that jar will slip off just so fine and smooth and easy." Chip-munk was spreading his hands flat on the floor in front of him as if he was smoothing a crumpled piece of paper. Cat was still well-was-seled, and he put out one paw to feel what it was that Chipmunk was smoothing. When he discovered that it was nothing, he was peeved.

"Will you quit that feely-fooling!" he snapped. "Trying to watch you talk with your paws makes my eyes swim." Chipmunk stuffed his paws into his pockets. "Besides that," yowled Cat, "you ain't making no sense. I know plenty of times that Rat has got himself into something that he couldn't get out of. Not backwards or buttered or any other way. And this looks like one of those times. We need a real method here."

"Why don't we just break the jar?'" asked Skunk, and before anyone could stop him, he stepped forward and hit the jar a good lick with his two-pound gravy ladle. Cat thought he heard Rat scream, but he couldn't be sure because the glass jar was ringing like a church chime on an icy cold morning. Rat's four paws were clenched together in a ball of toes, and his tail was snapping like a whip.

"Didn't break," said Skunk.

"Maybe it did," said Cat, thinking about Rat's head.

Dog leaned on the jar and rubbed his paw across it to make a squeaky sound. "You okay in there, Rat?" he yelled.

"Ooohhhhh!" moaned Rat.

"Move aside, Dog," said Skunk, "and I'll give it a double-hard hit." Skunk spit on his paws and lifted the ladle way back over his head to hit the jar with a crusher, but when he paused at the top of the stroke to take aim, Cat stepped up and snatched the ladle out of his paws. Skunk was so wrapped up in his swing that he didn't know the ladle was gone until he heaved forward to smack the jar.

Skunk swung hard and flipped himself over in a somersault. Chili powder flew everywhere. Everyone ran, except Rat, of course, to avoid being spiced as the cloud of chili powder drifted down. Lots of it fell on Skunk, who didn't really mind, but lots more of it fell on the Rat.

"Hack-cheep!" Rat sneezed. Normally, Rat had a good

strong-sounding sneeze, but with his head suck inside a glass jar, his sneezes had a bad quality.

"Hack-cheep!" he sneezed again. "Hack, hack, hack-CHEEP!"

Chipmunk came running from the kitchen with a big bowl of butter that he started to smear on Rat's neck. "This will do the..."

"Hack-cheep!"

"...trick, Rat. I know this will do it," said Chipmunk with a good rub of butter under Rat's chin.

"See here, Chipmunk," complained Cat, "you are making a buttery mess of Rat for no good purpose."

"No, no!" said Chipmunk, shaking his head like a bee was after his ear. "This will do it. This will really do it." He plopped another big gob of butter on Rat's shoulder.

Dog looked over Cat's head to see what Chipmunk was doing. He scratched his ear and then looked again. It didn't make sense to him. "Do you want me to get you a couple slices of bread, Chipmunk?" he asked.

"No," said Chipmunk. "I'm buttering Rat."

Dog couldn't see the purpose in that. "I guess we should get some jelly and pickles, huh?" he asked Cat.

"I'm going to go find Weasel and He-Otter," said Cat, and he left the room.

Skunk was still sitting on the floor after his tumble, and his head was going around in little circles. He was wasseled and dizzy and having trouble making his eyes see less than two or three of everything. He stood and walked over to where two Chipmunks were rubbing butter on three Rats.

"Hey, Chipmunk, if you can help me find my gravy ladle, I'll have Rat's head out of that jar in a couple whacks."

"Yep, yep, yep, yep!" said Chipmunk, bobbing his head. "But let's just try to slide him out of there with this butter first." Chipmunk's nose was running because of the chili powder, and when he tried to wipe it with his coat sleeve cuff he smeared some butter on his eyebrow.

Skunk did not think much of the sliding-Rat-out idea, but he figured that if Chipmunk was spreading butter on himself as well as on Rat, it might be a more complicated plan than he realized. He nodded his head and waited for Chipmunk to finish the buttering. If it didn't work, he could look for the ladle later.

Dog came down the spiral staircase with the Rabbits. All six of them. Still dressed in their clown costumes. They were all doing some rowdy running and jumping and hollering, and they were looking for more party excitement.

"There he is," Dog told that Rabbits as he pointed at Rat. "In big trouble."

"What'll we do?" asked the Rabbits, hopping all over poor old Rat and grabbing for prominent parts of him.

"We are going to pull his head out of that jar," explained Chipmunk with his hands covered in butter.

"Hoo-ray!" yelled the Rabbits, and they lifted Rat off the floor and arranged him for a good, hard, six-Rabbit pull.

"No!" said Chipmunk. "You can't pull the jar off his head all at once. He has to be more buttered-up so you can ease him out."

Dog picked up Rat's tail and handed it to Skunk. "Hold onto this tight and stay clear of the action," Dog told him.

"You betcha," said Skunk, and he took hold of Rat's tail and stood to the side.

"Arn nuffle luffle nerwin," mumbled Rat inside the jar as he felt himself being lifted by the Rabbits.

The two biggest Rabbits had hold of the jar, and one of them raised his paw to quiet the other four who had hold of Rat. "Now, we'll let her rip when I say 'HEAVE'!" he said. "Hoo-ray!" yelled the Rabbits. "We're ready!"

"No!" hollered Chipmunk.

Cat came into the front room with Weasel and He-Otter close behind. His eyes got big as saucers when he saw what was going on. "Hey! Stop! You Rabbits! Stop!" But it was too late.

"HEAVE!" ordered the big Rabbit.

"HEAVE!" yelled the rest of the Rabbits, and they all heaved.

"OOOHHHHH!" screamed Rat.

Then with a sound like a boot sucking out of thick mud, Rat's head popped out of the jar and everyone went flying in all directions. The two biggest Rabbits shot backwards across the room into Cat and Weasel and He-Otter, and they all crashed to the floor in a heap of teeth, claws and fur. The jar flew straight up, bounced off the ceiling, and landed on the toe of Chipmunk who commenced to stomp around the room like a bicycle with a flat tire. Rat's pants and the other four Rabbits smashed into the wall on the opposite side of the room, where they began to name-call and ear-bite one another. Rat and Skunk, who had kept a good tight grip on Rat's tail, whirled around seven times like a weather vane in a cyclone before they got tangled up with four or five onlookers and collapsed in a pile.

The whole house got real quiet. Cat sat up and slowly took a Rabbit's foot out of his pocket. Rat moaned from under a pile of clothes and animals. Chipmunk had his hurt toe in his mouth. Everyone was watching Cat with wide eyes.

Cat picked his seegar off the floor. It was mashed flat.

"I guess the party's over, huh?" asked Dog.

"Yes," said Cat. "Except for those who want to stay and dance the tango."

"What does that mean?" Lady Mouse whispered to Dog,

"It means trouble for anyone who stays," answered Dog.

Lady Mouse fidgeted. "Would you take me home now, Dog?" she whispered.

"Why sure," said Dog. They walked through the kitchen and stood outside by the cellar doors in the starlight.

"That was the first party I ever had," said Lady Mouse.

"Aw, that was nothing," said Dog with a wave of his paw. "You stick around with me and you'll see some real parties."

"Oh, I hope so!" said Lady Mouse. She kissed Dog on the tip of his nose and scurried down the cellar stairs.

"Hey!" said Dog, touching his nose. He shook his head. "Well what do you think about that?"

Dog walked back into the house as Cat was blowing out the last of the candles. Except for Rat's moaning and whining, everything was quiet. It had been some party.

Chapter 7
Rainy Day Friends

It was a dreary day. First fog, then clouds, then rain, then cold, then all of them together. Acting happy couldn't help. Everyone would know you were just acting, because nobody could be happy on this sort of day.

Scrawny Dog, Hungry Cat and Fat Rat were sitting in the front room of the Three-Story House feeling gloomy. Cat was drinking tea. Dog was fidgeting. Rat was worrying that he might catch pneumonia.

"I wanted to have a party tonight," whined Dog, "but who would come to a party on a day like this?"

"A duck…gulp…with…gulp…an umbrella," said Cat between gulps of hot raspberry tea.

"No one would go out in this rainstorm," said Dog. "Not even a duck. Not even a goose. Probably not even a fish."

"I used to go out and play in the rain," Rat said quietly.

Dog and Cat looked at him like he was a Rat without a lick of good sense.

"Why?" asked Dog.

"For fun," answered Rat.

"Yessir, yessir," chided Cat, holding his tea cup close to his face to warm his cold nose. "Sure is fun to get all wet."

"It is?" asked Dog.

"No!" said Cat.

"Well, why did you say that it is fun, then?"

Cat sighed. "That was just to make Rat feel stupid, Dog. It was irony. It was sarcasm. You wouldn't understand."

"I understand sour-cat-ism," said Dog. "You're a sour Cat most of the time. But that doesn't explain why Rat would want to go out and play in the rain. He whines a lot, but at least he ain't a sour-Cat." Cat gave Dog a sour look. "So tell us, Rat," continued Dog, "why did you used to go out in the rain?"

"Oh, when I was just a little Rat with lots of brothers and sisters, our mother would send us out to play in the rain with buckets."

Dog scratched his ears and made a sad face. "Didn't your mother like you, Rat?"

Rat gave Dog a hurt look. "Of course she did!" he snipped. "She liked us. She liked us a lot. She wanted us to have a good time."

"Having a good time meant sending you out in the rain to get soaking wet?" asked Cat.

"She didn't want us to get our clothes all wet, so she sent us out in our underwear and rubber boots," said Rat.

Dog and Cat looked sideways at Rat and then at each other. "And that was what you call fun?" asked Dog.

"It was fun," said Rat. "As best I remember, it was good fun."

"How could you possibly have fun in a rainstorm?" asked Cat.

"Why, we would fill up our buckets with rainwater and throw that water on each other as fast as we could. And we pushed each other down into the puddles and ran around and laughed and hollered."

"You call that a good time?" asked Cat. "I call that stupid."

"It was a good time," insisted Rat. "It was fun. It was some of the best fun I ever had."

"I think we should try it!" barked Dog.

"Then you better stop thinking, Dog," said Cat, "because we ain't going out in a driving rain and throw buckets of water on one another and laugh and holler and get pushed into puddles."

"But Rat says it was fun. He said it was good fun."

"Rat is stupid," said Cat. "It is no fun to be wet."

"Can't swim, huh?" Dog chided Cat.

"I can swim just fine."

"Afraid of water, huh?"

"No, I ain't afraid of water."

"Yes, you are," said Dog. "You're a Cat, and Cats are afraid of water."

Cat glared at Dog and gulped down the last of his tea from the cup.

"You're afraid that I'll throw too much water on you," Dog teased Cat. "And I would, too, because Dogs love water, and I can toss water faster than any Cat alive."

"Listen," growled Cat, "I ain't afraid of water, not one bit, and furthermore I can throw water better than you!"

"Yes you are, and no you can't," said Dog.

"Anyway," piped up Rat, "it isn't how fast you can throw water from a bucket, it's how good you throw it that counts. If I was throwing rainwater from a bucket, I could hit Cat with a gallon of it every throw, and he'd be one drowned-looking Cat."

Cat sputtered and spit. "I'm so quick that I could jump out of the way of any rainwater you throw at me, Rat!" he said. "And I'd soak you both soggy in one minute with the way I can throw buckets of water."

"Maybe you could if you weren't afraid of water," said Dog.

"I ain't afraid of water, Dog!"

"Yes, you are. You're a 'fraidy-Cat. 'Fraidy-Cat, 'fraidy-Cat!"

Cat clenched his jaw and set his teacup on the hearth of the fireplace. "Rat," he said slowly, "go get three buckets."

Rat walked into the kitchen and came back in a few minutes with three big empty tin cans. "We don't have three buckets," he told Dog and Cat. "We each get a tin can instead."

"That'll do," said Cat, snatching a tin can from Rat. He opened the front door wide. "By all means let us each take our respective tin cans and go outside into this driving rain and find out who is and who ain't afraid of water." He bowed low and with a sweep of his paw showed Dog that he should go first.

Dog walked out onto the porch and stuck his nose out from under the roof. "Wow!" he barked and jerked his head back. "That is a cold rain."

"It's going to get colder!" screeched Cat. He kicked Dog right on the tail, and Dog tumbled down the porch stairs into a deep puddle of rainwater. Quick as a flash, Cat jumped on Dog's back and was pouring cansful of water over his head.

"Hey, Cat!" yelled Rat.

"What?' asked Cat, looking up.

"This is what!" hollered Rat, and he threw a can of cold water into Cat's face. Then they were all three rolling in the cold rain puddle and calling each other names like sewer-Rat and 'fraidy-Cat and soggy-Doggy.

"Take that! Take that! Take that!" yelled Cat, throwing water like a fire hose.

"Stop it now! Stop it! I said STOP it!" Dog yelped at Cat while he held Rat by his coat collar and dipped him up and down in the deepest part of the puddle. Each time Rat came up he spit a mouthful of water on Dog and threw a can of water into Cat's face.

Pretty soon they were all tired of water fighting. They sat side-by-side in the cold puddle and looked at each other. Water was running off their chins and out of their ears. The rain was falling harder than ever. Cat threw his tin can onto the porch. "Well, are you satisfied, Dog?" he asked. "Are you satisfied that you got us all into a water fight?"

"Yep," said Dog.

"Well I'm n-n-not," chattered Rat. "I am n-n-not satisfied at all. I am w-w-wet and f-f-freezing c-c-cold."

"Rat," said Dog, "did your mother always make you do water fights like this and get freezing cold?"

"N-n-no," said Rat. "We only had water f-f-fights in the s-s-summertime."

Cat looked at his rain-soaked self and his soggy friends, put one paw on his head, closed his eyes, and sighed a sad little sigh through his wet whiskers. "Rat, you are so stupid," he said.

"W-w-well I'm s-s-smart enough to g-g-go back inside," replied Rat. He scrambled onto the porch and through the front door, and Dog and Cat followed close behind. They shivered into the front room, and Cat kicked the door shut. Rat looked the most miserable, but it wasn't because he was the wettest. It's just that Rats look bad wet.

"Yes, we are soaking wet," said Cat, dripping on the rug. "Look at this." He wrung out Dog's left ear with a hard twist and a pint of water ran out onto the floor. "Ooww!" yelped Dog as he swatted Cat's paws away. "Wring out your own wet ears, you dang Cat."

"I'm cold," whined Rat, pulling his wet coat around him and shivering.

"So you're cold, huh?' scolded Cat. "Should we feel sorry for you, Rat?"

"Yeah, Rat," said Dog. "Who was it that wanted us to run out in the rainstorm anyway? Was it me, the Dog? No! Was it him, the Cat? No! Was it you, the Rat? Yes, yes it was. It was you. And now who's whining about being wet and cold?"

"Me," whined Rat. "Let's light a big fire in the fireplace and get warm."

"Ain't got no wood," said Cat as he searched in his unwettest pocket for a seegar.

"Go outside and get some firewood, Dog," said Rat.

"Me! Beans to that, Rat!" yelped Dog. "Beans to that is what I say. I'm not drowning myself for firewood. Not for nobody."

"Make sure to get dry firewood, Dog," said Cat, striking a match and trying to light a damp seegar. "Wet firewood won't burn, so get some that's dry."

"No, I say! Beans to that!" said Dog. "I'm not going back out into the cold rain, and that's that." He stomped his feet on the floor to show he intended to keep them right there.

"Well then let's wrap up in a blanket," said Rat. "Pretty soon I'm going to have a sneezing fit if I don't get warm. And a sneezing fit is just one step from pneumonia."

Cat was blowing on his seegar, trying to dry it. "Whose blanket?" he asked.

"Not mine," said Rat. "You two would get it all wet."

Cat and Dog both gave Rat sour-Cat-ism looks.

"I guess we can wrap up in my blanket," said Dog.

"I'm not wrapping up in your blanket, Dog," said Rat. "Your blanket is too dirty."

"You are the whiniest Rat I ever knew," scolded Cat. "I suppose you want to wrap your soggy rodent self in my blanket."

"Thanks, Cat. I sure do," said Rat, and he ran across the room as fast as his four feet could go and leaped into Cat's big brown chair.

"Hey! Hey there! Stop there!" yelled Cat with a drippy wave of his paw. "Don't put your greasy, wet self in my dry chair, Rat. Do you hear me, Rat?"

"Well, I'm not going to sit here on the floor in a cold puddle," said Dog. "I'm going to wrap up in your blanket with Rat." He trotted across the room leaving puddles big as pancakes behind him.

"You two better keep out of my chair!" yowled Cat, but the only answer he heard was the creak and squeak of the chair's springs. "Well if that don't ice the biscuits," sputtered Cat as he stalked across the room. He looked into his chair and, sure enough, there were Rat and Dog with his blanket pulled so high around them that only their ears and tips of their noses showed. Cat put a paw over one eye and snarled.

"You might as well get in and wrap up with us Cat," mumbled Rat. "Your blanket's all wet anyhow."

"But it sure is warm," added Dog.

"Such dear, dear friends," sassed Cat with a big wide-eyed face, "to help me share my good fortune of a dry, clean, warm blanket on such a foul weather day."

"Yeah," agreed Dog.

Cat sighed and climbed into the chair and snuggled into the blanket between Dog and Rat. It was warm. Cozy warm. "I guess having good pals is more important than having a dry blanket," said Cat.

Dog was getting sleepy. "Yeah," he said, "that's more important." Cat looked at him a long minute and then pinched his ear just as he was about to drop off to sleep. "Mumpf!" mumpfed Dog looking at Cat through squinty eyes. Cat bopped Dog on the nose with his paw. Then they all settled back to take a nap.

"Zzzzzzzzzzzzzzzz," they snored, all tucked into the warm blanket in the warm chair.

Something bumped against the front door. Thump, thump!

Rat woke up and moaned. "Oh, no."

"What's that bumping against the door?" asked Cat.

"It's bad news, that's what it is," said Rat. "Bad news come to call right in the middle of a nice nap."

"It's just someone knocking on the door," yawned Dog.

The bump bumped again. Three times.

"It's probably someone big and nasty and awful," said Rat, grabbing his tail and twisting it into a knot. Dog shook his head. "Rat, you get nervouser and nervouser every day. It's probably somebody nice and friendly."

"Then why don't he just come in instead of making them scary thumping and bumping noises at the door?" asked Rat. "It's got to be trouble. We all know it."

"We might as well see who it is," said Cat. They all tumbled out of the chair and walked to the door. Cat pulled it open. Rat and Dog stood behind him and looked over his shoulder. They saw someone standing on the porch. A bird. A white bird. He was holding a suitcase by the handle and was about to bump it against the door again just as Cat opened it. He stopped in mid-bump. Dog, Cat and Rat eyed the bird. The bird eyed Dog, Cat and Rat. No one said a word.

"Cat got your tongue?" the bird finally said to Dog. Dog looked suspiciously at Cat and put his paw in his mouth to check that he still had his tongue. He took a closer look at the bird.

"Nice coat you got there," Dog said. "Gray and white. Colorful."

"Thanks," said the bird. "Mind if I hop inside? It's raining out here you know." He had a beady black eye. Dog figured he had another one just like it on the other side of his head.

"Don't you like the rain?" Dog asked, poking Rat in the ribs with his elbow. "Rat here likes the rain. He thinks it's fun to play out in the rain."

"It's alright, I suppose," said the bird. "We have better rain where I come from."

"Oh, yeah?" said Cat, a bit perturbed. "And where would that be?"

"The coast, my good Cat," said the bird. He fished around in his coat pocket. "My card," he said, handling a little square of paper to Cat. Cat read it aloud:

C.Gull

Highly Known Author

A Bird On His Way Up

All three of them looked at the little picture of a flying bird on the back of the card. "Do you have forty-seven more of these?" asked Dog.

"I might," beamed C.Gull. "What would be the object of such a copious quantity?"

"Huh?" said Dog.

"I think he means, why do you need so many of them," Rat told Dog.

"Oh," said Dog. "To make a pea-knuckle card deck. We like to play pea-knuckle."

Gull got real quiet. The rain started falling harder. "So, may I come in?" asked Gull, shaking water from his hat. "It's been a long flight."

"Oh, please do," said Cat with a little bow. "Ought we to roll out the red carpet for you?"

"No, no, no! Heavens no," said Gull, hopping into the front room.

"I wouldn't want to disrupt the homey atmosphere of this place. Wouldn't change a single facet of it." He set down his suitcase and Cat closed the door behind him.

"So, what's your pleasure, Gull?" Dog asked him.

"I beg your pardon?" said Gull

"You don't have to beg for it around here," said Dog. "It's yours for the asking."

Gull didn't know what to say to that. He looked as if he might start to mumble and mutter, so Rat said, "Dog means, what can we do for you?"

"Ah, yes. I understand," said Gull. "Well, my reputable and esteemed trio, here is my proposition." Gull took a thin brown cigarette out of his pocket, stuck it into his beak, lit it with a wooden match, flipped back the tail of his coat, and put one foot on his suitcase."

"Bravo!" cheered Dog.

"I beg your pardon?" said Gull.

"You don't have to beg…" started Dog.

"I mean," interrupted Gull, "why did you cheer 'bravo'?"

"Bravo for your propped-position," said Dog. "Well done. Nice boots, too. Orange. They go right with your coat."

"Why, thank you," said Gull, flipping a gob of mud off one boot with his wingtip. "But I'm not here to demonstrate a propped-position but to offer a proposition to you folks, which I am sure you will want to hear in greatest detail." He took a deep pull on his cigarette, but most of the smoke shot out through the nose holes of his beak.

Everyone was quiet.

"Would you like to hear it?" asked Gull.

Cat was looking cross-eyed at a bent whisker on his nose. Rat was twisting his tail and watching a bug crawl across the floor. Dog was singing a song to himself and wagging his tail to keep time.

"I said, would you like to hear it?" Gull asked again.

"Sure," answered Cat. "We're all ears."

"Gents," lectured Gull with a sweep of his wing, "I am, as you know from my card, an author. No doubt you have heard of my first short novel entitled *The Sea Boomed Skyward*, by C. Gull, which many top-flight literary agents considered recommending to publishers." Gull had a misty, faraway look in his eyes.

"Was it in the newspapers?" asked Rat

"Oh, yes," said Gull. "Several mentioned it."

"We don't read the newspapers," said Cat.

"That's probably why we haven't heard of it," said Dog. "But if we ever get a copy, we'll be sure to put it on the shelf."

"Of course, of course," said Gull, hardly listening. "But to get to the point, I am now in the midst of another great work." He touched his wingtip gently against a pocket on the side of his suitcase. "And I'm quite willing to do honor to this house by living here for a month, or perhaps two or three, while I complete this magnificent book."

"Is that a fact," said Cat.

"Yes, yes," said Gull flipping ashes from his cigarette onto the floor. "I'm quite willing."

"Oh, dear," moaned Rat.

"No room," said Cat.

"Perhaps you have concerns about my sincerity," said Gull. "I have here a detailed letter of reference from a highly respected family of Pelicans." He handed the letter to Dog. "They live on the coast, you know. I stayed with them six weeks while I finished my first book. It's dedicated to them. As my next one could be dedicated to you, my fine Dog, Cat and Rat."

Dog looked at the letter. "I sure wish I could read fancy writing like this," he said with a sad shake of his head. "And I always did want to meet a Pelican. Did you know, Cat, that a Pelican can put as much food in its mouth as in its stomach? Why you could eat breakfast in one bite, and lunch would just be a swallow away."

"And that," said Gull, "is perhaps the least of their numerous talents."

"Listen, Gull," said Cat, "let's get this straight. We got enough feathery folks around here, and we ain't looking for more."

"Ah," said Gull with a smug chuckle, "I could best answer that comment with a smug chuckle. You see, I am not your average bird."

"No room," growled Cat.

"But surely in such a big house…"

"Full."

"Perhaps in the cellar…"

"Junk Mice."

"Or the third floor…"

"Birds."

"A small closet on the second floor…"

"Rabbits."

"Any room at all."

"All full."

"All?"

"Full!"

"My dear Cat, I must insist," said Gull, stamping his foot on the floor. "I simply cannot allow you to pass up this opportunity."

Cat unbuttoned the cuffs of his shirt sleeves. "Dog, go to the kitchen and get me the salt shaker," he said, looking hard at Gull through narrowed eyes.

"Here," said Dog, handing the envelope back to Gull. "You better get a good hold onto everything you don't want to lose." He turned and headed for the kitchen. "You want the big salt shaker, Cat?" he asked.

"Yep, bring me the big one," said Cat. "This bird looks like he could use a lot of salt on his tail."

"Surely we can be reasonable," Gull said to Cat.

"We surely can," agreed Cat, spitting on the knuckles of his left paw.

C.Gull looked at Dog as he disappeared through the kitchen door. He looked at Rat who was sitting on the floor and twisting his tail and saying "Oh, my! Oh, my!" He looked at Cat. Twice. "Well, thank you for your time, gents," Gull said, "but I really must fly. He put on his hat and picked up his suitcase. Rat opened the door for him as he waddled out.

"Some Gull," said Cat, buttoning his sleeve cuffs.

Dog came back into the front room carrying the big salt shaker and watched as Gull walked off the porch and out into the rain. "If it don't rain tomorrow," he said, "maybe we can have a party, and I'll invite Lady Mouse."

"Or even if it does rain," said Rat.

Chapter 8
Lady Mouse And Dog And Rat

"Tonight, Lady Mouse, we are having a dinner party," said Dog, standing on the bottom step of the cellar stairs and opening his eyes wide to see Lady Mouse in the dim light.

"A dinner party?" said Lady Mouse. "What do you do at a dinner party?"

"First you eat," explained Dog, "and then you do the same things that you do at any other party."

"Well, I shall certainly come," said Lady Mouse. "Thank you for inviting me. What time should I be there?"

"Right now," replied Dog. "Skunk is fixing grub in the kitchen for the party dinner."

"Oh, Dog!" said Lady Mouse, getting pale around the eyes. "I'm not even dressed up for a party dinner."

"You don't have to look pretty for it, you just have to eat it," said Dog. "Come on, or we'll be late." He led Lady Mouse up the cellar stairs and they went into the kitchen.

Skunk was standing on a chair by the stove cooking a huge pot full of something. "This," he said with a stir of his spoon, "shall be a culinary delight beyond compare." He kissed his fingertips and stroked back his hair under his chef's hat. All of the Three-Story House folks were crowded into the kitchen, and those closest to the stove were trying to look into Skunk's bubbling pot of grub.

"What did you say it's called?" asked Chipmunk, leaning against a leg of Skunk's chair.

"I didn't say what it's called, actually," said Skunk as he stirred with big round swashes that made gravy slosh over the rim of the pot.

"Well, what are you going to call it?" asked Chipmunk, getting ready to taste a drop of gravy with the tip of his tongue.

"Haven't thought of a real flashy sounding name for this entrée yet," replied Skunk with a dreamy look in his eyes, "so maybe I'll just call it 'green toadstool fungus stew, with hints of nutmeg and cinnamon.'"

 Chipmunk's tongue stopped in mid-lick.

"Did you say 'green toadstool'?" asked Rat.

"Yes, I did," said Skunk with another stir.

"Did you say 'fungus'?" asked Cat with a gulp.

"Yes, I did."

"You did say 'nutmeg and cinnamon,' didn't you?" asked Dog.

"Yes, I did," said Skunk again, and he dipped out a spoonful of red-brown-green-yellow gravy and lowered it down in front of Rat's face. "Want to be the first to sample it, Rat?" he asked.

Rat clamped both paws over his mouth so fast he fell onto his fat behind. "No famk que," he mumbled through his toes.

"Cat?" asked Skunk, swinging the spoon around toward Cat's face.

"Skunk?" asked Cat, pushing the spoon right back.

"Don't you want a taste?" asked Skunk.

"Don't you want a taste?" Cat asked right back.

"Do you know what you're missing?" asked Skunk, with a snooty look.

"Greasy frog-seat funny goo," said Cat.

"Green toadstool fungus stew, with hints of nutmeg and cinnamon," corrected Skunk. "Good grub, and a one-of-a-kind concoction."

"None for me," said Cat.

"None?" asked Skunk.

"Not a drop, not a drip, not a dribble," said Cat.

"What are you going to do for party dinner?" asked Skunk.

"I don't know about anyone else," said Cat, "but I will do with other or do without."

Chipmunk started jumping around the kitchen and pulling at his ears. "I don't care what Cat says," he screeched. "I'm not eating any of the green goo stuff! No sir, not one bite."

"Me neither," said Dog.

"Well, who does want a big dish of stew?" asked Skunk, looking at all the faces turned toward him. "I assure you it is dee-licious." Nobody seemed eager to step up and get a bowl.

"I guess no one is that hungry," said Weasel.

Skunk's mouth fell open and he stood there with a gabberflasted look on his face. He threw his paws up in the air, and greasy gobs of green gravy flew off the spoon and spattered on the ceiling.

"Well, isn't this a fine kettle of fish!" Skunk scolded everyone in the kitchen.

"Huh!" Cat whispered to Rat. "I wish it was."

"I cook and cook and cook my stripe off, and what thanks do I get for it? When does anyone ever give my cooking any consideration at all?" Skunk was really worked up. He yanked off his chef's hat and threw it onto the table, and he clamped down the lid on the stew pot. Clang! "Mean-mouthed, that's what I get! Never a single 'Thank you, Skunk' or 'Good grub, Skunk'! No sir, never. Not once! Not ever!

"You folks just think you know everything that's good. You won't ever try anything that's new or different. You all think you're so smart about food. Well, I'll tell you this much: you ain't smart about good food. In fact you don't know nothin' about what's good food and what's not good food.

"Okay then, fine!" he said, taking off his apron. "Old Skunk isn't cooking himself to death for you. You just see if I ever cook again! Because I am never, ever cooking anything for any you, never, ever again!"

Skunk said that about once a week.

Dog was prowling around inside the kitchen cupboards. "Who wants to eat graham crackers and applesauce?" he asked.

Everyone looked one last time at the pot of green toadstool stew on the stovetop.

"I do," said Rat. "I want some graham crackers and applesauce."

"We do, too," said He-Otter and She-Otter.

"I want a graham cracker," said Bluebird.

"Me, too," agreed Nuthatch.

"I love applesauce," chattered Chipmunk. "Absolutely love it. One of my favorite foods, whatever it is. Can I have some sugar sprinkled on it?"

"I'm going to the Dump to find something to eat," said Cat. "Anyone want to come with me?"

"I'll go with you," said Weasel.

"Eat at the Dump!" cheered the Rabbits. "Last one there is a skinny Rabbit!" They ran out the back door and down the stairs.

"Let's eat in the front room," Dog said to Lady Mouse and the Birds and Chipmunk and everyone else. They all grabbed plates and followed Dog out of the kitchen, leaving Skunk, Fool Owl, and a ten-quart pot full of green toadstool fungus stew, with hints of nutmeg and cinnamon. Skunk watched them go and lifted his nose for a noble look at Owl.

"That, Owl, is the respect an adventurous cook gets for his attempts at creativity in the culinary arts," said Skunk. He lifted the lid from the pot, skimmed off a spoonful of green gravy, and offered it to Owl. "Would you care for a taste?"

Fool Owl took a hasty step backward. "I just remembered I promised the junk Mice that I would dine with them some evening this month," he said, "and this seems to be a good night to fulfill that promise."

Skunk looked at the greasy green gravy in the spoon, tossed it back into the stew pot, and wiped his hands on his pants. "I think I'll go with you, Owl," he said. "I wouldn't want to be greedy and eat all of this grub before anyone else gets a taste. Besides, it will be just as good tomorrow." They headed for the cellar to find the junk Mice.

In the front room folks were crunching on graham crackers and slurping applesauce while Dog built a fire in the fireplace to make wassel. Lady Mouse was sitting in the brown chair, and Rat walked over to her with a tin can in each of his paws.

"Lady Mouse," he said in a real shy voice as he held out a tin can to her, "would you sit by the fire with me tonight while we all drink wassel?"

Lady Mouse gave Rat a funny-faced look. "No, Rat. I am going to sit by the fire with Dog."

"Oh," said Rat. They both looked at the tin can he was holding out in his paw. He let it fall to his side. "That's fine, I guess."

Lady Mouse slid down out of the chair, and as she walked across the room she turned her head and gave Rat that same funny-faced look again. Rat felt all hollow inside and didn't want his graham cracker.

Dog had a fire roaring in the fireplace. "I'll get the bucket," he announced, "and everyone else should get the fixings for the wassel." Folks scrambled every which way to find stuff.

Rat walked out the front door, hopped down the stairs and headed for the Dump, partly to search for apples for the wassel, but mostly to search for Cat. He found him sitting on a truck tire eating a can of tuna. Rat sat down beside him and sighed a quiet little sigh.

"What's the matter, Rat?" asked Cat, wiping some fishy oil off his whiskers with the back of his paw.

"Cat," sighed Rat again, "do you think Lady Mouse is pretty?"

Cat thought a minute. "I suppose so. For a Mouse."

"I think she is awfully pretty," sighed Rat. "Maybe the prettiest Mouse I've ever seen."

Cat gave Rat a funny-faced look, almost exactly the same look as the one that Lady Mouse gave him when he was talking to her in the brown chair.

"Do you think, Cat," asked Rat, "that a pretty Lady Mouse could like an old Fat Rat?"

"I don't know, Rat," answered Cat. "You better ask her."

"Maybe I will," said Rat. "I wonder if she would tell me."

Cat stood up and threw the empty tuna can onto a trash pile. "Let's get back to the party, Rat, where I won't have to hear anymore of this stupid Rat-talk about you and Lady Mouse."

Rat was walking with stars in his eyes all the way back to the Three-Story House. Cat had to pick him up three times after he tripped and fell down because he wasn't watching his steps.

"Now listen, Rat," Cat scolded, "if you fall one more time, you can lie there the rest of the night because I am not picking you up again. You act like you already had too many cans of wassel."

"I'll be more careful, Cat," promised Rat. Then he tripped and fell on the stairs.

"Hey! There's my pals," hollered Dog as Cat and Rat walked into the front room. He was sitting with Lady Mouse on the rug in front of the fireplace, and he waved a big happy wave at Cat and Rat. Lady Mouse looked at them and tried to smile a little. Cat and Rat each got a can of wassel from the bucket and sat on the floor. Cat lit a seegar.

"I'm going to smoke my pipe," said Dog. He reached into the deepest pocket inside his coat and pulled out a big white and silver smoking pipe. "Got any 'baccer, Cat?" he asked.

"Nope," answered Cat, "only seegars."

"Well then, I'll have to smoke my own," said Dog. He took a gray paper bag out of another pocket. He stuck the pipe stem in his mouth, jerked it right back out, crossed his eyes, spit twice, stuck out his tongue, and wiped his nose.

"What's wrong?" asked Rat.

"My pipe's still got a bit of soap in her, I reckon," said Dog.

"How did soap get in your pipe?" asked Rat.

"From blowing bubbles," said Dog. "I use it for a soap bubble pipe."

Cat took his seegar out of his mouth and glared at Dog. "You were going to put my good 'baccer in a soap bubble pipe?"

"You got some 'baccer?" asked Dog.

Cat put his seegar back in his mouth, squinted his eyes at Dog, scratched his ear, and yowled, "Bubbles!"

"Not bubbles," said Dog. "'Baccer."

"No, and even if I did have some, I wouldn't give it to you to put in your dang soap bubble pipe," said Cat.

"Then I'll have to use my own," Dog said again, and he packed the bowl of the pipe full of 'baccer from the gray paper bag. He reached into his pocket again, took out a gold automatic pipe lighter, and handed it to Rat. "Light that for me, would you Rat?"

Rat took the lid off. There was an oily rag stuck into the top of the automatic pipe lighter, and when he held it near the burning log in the fireplace it went poof! and started to flame. Rat handed it back to Dog, and Dog lit the 'baccer in the bowl of his pipe with it. He burned his paw when he clamped the lid back on.

Cat knew this was too complicated. "Why don't you just use a match, Dog?"

Dog held the automatic pipe lighter in front of Cat's face. "Because I got an automatic pipe lighter. You don't ever need to use a match if you got an automatic pipe lighter." He took a deep suck on the stem of his pipe as he put the lighter back into his pocket, and he blew out a big cloud of gray stinky pipe smoke. "Want to see me do some smoke tricks, Cat?" he asked.

"No," said Cat.

"Rat, do you want to see me do some smoke tricks?" asked Dog.

"I don't care," said Rat, who was busy watching Lady Mouse as if she were the only other person at the party.

"Then watch carefully," said Dog. He half-shut his eyes and took another deep suck on the stem of his pipe. He blew out a puff of smoke shaped like an 'O' and watched it float up to the ceiling.

"That's an 'O'," he explained to Rat. "Now watch be blow an 'M' for Mouse." He blew another "O."

"Now watch me blow a 'C' for Cat." He blew another "O."

"Now watch me blow a 'Z' for…"

"Hey, Dog!" interrupted Cat.

"What?" asked Dog.

"How many of these smoke tricks do you do?"

"Not counting specials and doubles, I'd say about seventy-one," said Dog.

"Well, don't blow them all tonight."

"Okay" said Dog, here's the last one." He took a suck on the stem of his pipe and blew out a huge 'Z' that floated across the room and blurred to a smoky cloud right before Cat's nose. Cat's tail shot straight out like a bolt, and the hair on his ears stood up.

"Dang!" he yowled. "Did you see that, Rat?"

"See what?" asked Rat, still looking dreamily at Lady Mouse.

"That smoke 'Z' that Dog just blew."

"A smoke sea?" mumbled Rat who wasn't paying much attention to anything but Lady Mouse. "A sea is made of water, Cat, not smoke."

Cat started to explain and then stopped. "Never mind, Rat. It couldn't have happened. Do you want some more wassel?"

"Sure," said Rat.

"Then go get a can for both of us," said Cat, and he handed Rat two tin cans.

Rat filled the cans with wassel from the bucket and thought what a nice dinner party it was. Everyone was here, even the third floor birds and the Rabbits, but it was a quiet party. The kind of party Cat liked and Dog didn't. The fireplace was burning low, the room was smoky, folks were talking, and Weasel was over in the far corner teaching Chipmunk a funny song about Gophers.

"Let's all sing," suggested Bluebird. "I have a guitar upstairs."

"Oh no," moaned Dog.

"You hush, Dog," said Bluebird. "I know a nice song titled 'A Sweet Bird Makes a House a Home.' I'll get my guitar, and Quail and I will teach it to everyone." Bluebird hopped toward the spiral staircase.

Dog started to fidget. He stood up and looked around the room. "Hey, Rabbits!" he barked.

"What?" asked the Rabbits.

"Let's go down to the River."

"Hoo-ray!" shouted the Rabbits. "We're going down to the River!"

Lady Mouse tugged at Dog's pant cuff. "Dog," she whispered. "Oh, Dog."

"What?" asked Dog, looked down over his shoulder at Lady Mouse.

"Why don't you stay here with me?"

"Because I don't want to sing."

Lady Mouse thought a moment. "Can I go to the River with you?" she asked.

"Oh, no," said Dog. "The River is no place for a lady."

"Well, what should I do?"

"Learn Bluebird's song, I guess," suggested Dog. He hitched up his pants. "Come on, Rabbits," he yelled.

"Hoo-ray!" cheered the Rabbits again. "Last one to the River is a wet Rabbit!" They scrambled out of the front door with Dog close behind.

"But, Dog…," squeaked Lady Mouse.

"See you later!" barked Dog with a wave of his paw, and he was gone.

Rat watched Dog run out through the door, and then he looked at Lady Mouse. She had a little tear in each eye. It made Rat feel awful.

He cleared his throat with a "Hurrumph," stood up, and walked over to Lady Mouse by the fireplace. "Let me get you another can of wassel, Lady Mouse," he said. He took her can and his and filled them from the bucket. When he came back, the tears were gone from her eyes, but she still looked sad.

"Do you want to hear a story?" Rat asked her.

"A story?" asked Lady Mouse. "What kind of story?"

"A story about Dog and Cat and me when we lived in the City."

"All right," said Lady Mouse, who did not know much about the City.

"It's a story about Box Mice," started Rat, and he told her the story of the crushed cardboard box, the Mouse, the hatpin, and his hurt ribs. At first she could only smile, but when Rat told her the part about the Mouse yelling "Nyah! Nyah! Nyah!" with the hatpin, she laughed and laughed.

"Is it that funny?" asked Rat, happy to hear Lady Mouse laughing.

"No," said Lady Mouse. "You just tell it funny."

"I know another one," said Rat.

"Why don't we go sit in the brown chair, and you can tell it to me," said Lady Mouse. She took him by the paw, led him to the chair, climbed in, and scooted over to make room for him to sit beside her. Rat looked around. Cat was drinkng wassel with Weasel by the fire. Dog was long gone to the River with the Rabbits. Bluebird and Quail were arguing about a song and playing tug-o-war with the guitar. Rat didn't know what to do. He climbed into the brown chair and sat beside Lady Mouse, but it didn't seem right.

"What is your next story about?" asked Lady Mouse, taking hold of his paw again.

Rat tried hard to remember another story. "Our ride in a truck to the Dump," he said. He told her that story and two more. Lady Mouse liked them all. When he finished the last one, Rat noticed that almost all the folks were gone from the front room.

"It must be late," Rat said to Lady Mouse. "Probably I should walk you home."

"Why, thank you, Rat," said Lady Mouse. She set her wassel can on the arm of the brown chair and hopped down onto the floor. Rat slid off the chair, and they walked together through the kitchen and out to the cellar stairs.

"Thank you for walking me home, Rat, and thank you for the funny stories," said Lady Mouse.

"You're welcome," said Rat. "I like to tell funny stories. I got a hundred of them to tell you." He looked into Lady Mouse's pretty eyes. They were soft and round and big and brown and made his tummy feel warmer than wassel. So what did he do? He took her by the paw and kissed her right on the end of her nose!

"Oh, my," said Lady Mouse, and her face turned red and then pale.

"W-well, I b-better get b-back into the house," stammered Rat. "G-good-night, Lady Mouse."

"Good-night," Rat, she said softly. "I'll see you at the next party."

"Oh, sure," said Rat with a happy grin. Then he couldn't think of anything else to say, so he scurried up the stairs. As he closed the cellar doors, Rat's feet were on the ground but his eyes were way up in the stars. He turned around, tripped, and fell down on his fat tummy.

Chapter 9
The River

It seemed the winter would stay away forever. The weather turned warmer, the days were sunny, and everyone at the Three-Story House thought things were fine. A few quiet days went by before Dog commenced to wish for another party. The evening was so right! That's what he said to Cat when he asked if they could have a party that very night – a quiet one, of course. Cat said it would be okay, and Dog headed for the cellar to invite Lady Mouse.

"Another party?" asked Lady Mouse. "Is that all you ever do, Dog?"

"Whenever I can," said Dog. "You going to come?"

"I don't know," said Lady Mouse fluffing her ears and pointing her nose in the air away from Dog. "You didn't show me a very nice time at the last party."

Now about this time, Rat came walking through the backyard twilight with a white clover flower in one paw and a warm glow in his tummy. He was going to ask Lady Mouse to go for a walk with him along the River, but just as he put his foot on the top step of the cellar stairway, he heard Dog talking with her.

"That was the last party," Dog was explaining to Lady Mouse. "I didn't want to sing no Bluebird song, and the Rabbits are real fun at the River. Real fun."

"I wouldn't know, never having been invited to go to the River" replied Lady Mouse, keeping her nose high in the air like she was looking at something important on the plumbing pipes overhead.

"Huh?" asked Dog.

"You told me I couldn't go to the River with you," Lady Mouse reminded him.

"Oh," said Dog, remembering. "But that was the last party. This time I'll spend the whole party with you. I'll show you a good time! Who else can party like me?"

"I don't have to go to the party with you, you know," huffed Lady Mouse. "I can always go with Rat. He was very nice to me at the last party."

"Rat!" barked Dog. "Why, Rat is no fun at a party. All he does is mumble and whine."

"Maybe he's not much fun," said Lady Mouse, "but at least he doesn't run off to the River with those rowdy Rabbits."

"That was the last party," insisted Dog. "That won't happen at this party."

"Besides," said Lady Mouse, "Rat told me some very nice stories. Funny stories."

"Told stories!" chided Dog. "A party is for making stories, not telling stories."

"They were very nice stories," said Lady Mouse. "Nicer than any stories you've ever told me."

"I never told you any stories," said Dog.

"That's exactly what I'm talking about," snipped Lady Mouse.

"Listen," said Dog, "you come to this party with me, and you'll have a better time than any story. Stick with me, and you can do whatever I do, even go to the River."

"With the Rabbits?" asked Lady Mouse.

Dog thought a minute. "Maybe," he said.

"Well, if I go to this party with you, and I'm not saying for sure that I will go to this party with you, I'll have to wear my yellow boots and green stockings," said Lady Mouse.

"You don't need no yellow boots and green socks," said Dog. "We got to get started."

"I said I am going to wear my yellow boots and green stockings, Dog, and that is what I intend to do. So you just sit there on the step and wait while I find them and put them on. Then maybe I will go to the party with you."

Rat heard all of this talk between Dog and Lady Mouse, and it faded the warm feeling in his tummy faster than swallowing an ice cube. He looked at the clover flower in his paw and wished he had never picked it and had never come to the cellar to ask Lady Mouse to go for a walk. And while he was standing there with his head hanging down feeling sorry for himself, all of a sudden here came Dog and Lady Mouse up the cellar stairs! Rat shoved the clover flower into his pants pocket, jumped behind the bushes, and put his front paws over his eyes to make himself invisible. Dog and Lady Mouse came out through the cellars doors and headed for the kitch-en.

"There's still some blueberry soda," Dog was saying to Lady Mouse as they walked together. "You and me can drink a bottle of it, Lady Mouse, while the wassel is fixing."

They went up the back stairs and into the kitchen, and Rat was left in the bushes feeling awful. He didn't know what to do. He didn't ever want to go to another party. He sat on the top step of the cellar stairway and looked down into the dark. The smashed clover flower made a big bulge in his pocket.

Well, Rat thought to himself with a sad little sigh, I could leave the clover flower in the cellar for Lady Mouse and go for a walk by myself along the River. Maybe I will see her tomorrow, and maybe she will know the clover flower was from me.

Inside the Three-Story House, Cat was searching for Rat. He knew Rat had been acting funny the past few days, and he was starting to worry that Rat might be going winter crazy. Winter crazy is when the short, dark winter days and the cold and snowy wintry weather makes you do odd things and think odd thoughts. It's why bears and groundhogs go off and hibernate.

Dog was standing in the kitchen opening a bottle of blueberry soda, and Cat hoped he would know something about Rat's whereabouts. "Dog," he asked, "where is the Rat?"

Dog did not pay any attention to Cat because he was trying to get a wad of bubble gum from behind his ear. He had put it there earlier for safekeeping, and it was stuck in his fur real good. "Dog, I asked you, where is the Rat?" Cat said again, louder this time, and he gave Dog a poke in the ear with his elbow that mashed the bubble gum farther into his fur.

"What did you do that for?" Dog barked at Cat, working on the gum wad with both front paws.

"So your furry ear would stick open and you would hear what I say," yowled Cat. "Now I am asking you one last time: do you know where is the Rat?"

"Well, I ain't sure...," hemmed and hawed Dog.

"...but you got an idea," finished Cat.

"Yeah, I got an idea."

"And what idea have you got?"

"Rat might have gone to the cellar to see Lady Mouse."

"How come?"

"He was probably going to ask her to come with him to the party, but she isn't going to be in the cellar when he gets there," snickered Dog with an I-know-why grin on his face. He gave a double-hard tug on the wad of bubble gum and it came out from behind his ear in a ragged, furry chunk. Dog took a look at it and popped it into his mouth.

"Why isn't she going to be in the cellar when Rat goes to invite her to the party?" asked Cat.

Dog was doing some noisy chewing on his wad of furry bubble gum and looking thoughtful. "I think there is too much fur in this gum, Cat," he said. "It keeps breaking into bits and parts when I chew it. Bubble gum isn't supposed to break into bits and parts. It's supposed to stick together in one chewy lump."

Cat walked a fast circle around Dog and started to mutter. He whipped a seegar out of his vest pocket, lit it, and stood there smoking at Dog. Then he reached up and took a big cast iron skillet off the stovetop.

"Dog," said Cat, running one paw over the flat, hard bottom of the skillet, "talking to you always makes me feel like I'm in a hurry. I can't exactly understand why that is, Dog, because I ain't in a hurry. But right now I feel like I got to have an exact answer from you in exactly five seconds, and I want to point out to you that if you do not tell me exactly what I want to know by the time I count exactly to five, I am going to lamblast the flat of this cast iron skillet exactly across the top of your breakable head."

Dog looked at the skillet and tried to think straight and fast.

"Two," counted Cat.

"What happened to 'one'?" asked Dog.

"Three," counted Cat.

Dog took the wad of bubble gum out of his mouth. "Rat probably went to see Lady Mouse in the cellar to ask her to come to the party with him," said Dog, talking as fast as he could talk, "because he sat with her in the big brown chair at the last party and told her stories while I was at the River with the Rabbits, and don't you think that was kind of a dirty Rat-trick, Cat, to tell her funny stories about us three when I wasn't there?"

Cat thought about that for one second. "Four," he said, raising the skillet.

Dog gulped. "Anyhow, Lady Mouse isn't going to be in the cellar because I went down there and asked her first to come to the party with me, and now she is in the front room watching the wassel cooking while I'm getting us a bottle of blueberry soda." Dog held up the bottle of blueberry soda for Cat to see.

Cat threw the cast iron skillet back onto the stovetop with a crash and a clatter. He smoked hard on his seegar and thought harder. "Stories, huh?" he said to Dog.

"Yeah," said Dog. "Lots of them."

"Well," said Cat, "maybe Rat is not going winter crazy after all. Maybe he is just stupid."

"I'm going to go get me some wassel," said Dog, popping the furry bubble gum back into his mouth and picking up a tin can.

"Good idea," said Cat with a sour look at Dog. "Go get yourself a can of wassel. Don't do anything about Rat and you and Lady Mouse, just go get some wassel."

"Well, maybe I will," said Dog with a huff and a sniff.

"Sure you will. Of course you will," yowled Cat as he walked out the back door.

"Well, maybe I will!" Dog said again, but Cat was gone and didn't hear him.

When Cat walked down the cellar stairway, Rat was sitting on a wooden box by the coal bin. He held the white clover flower in his paw, but when he heard someone coming down the steps he stuffed it back into his pocket where it couldn't be seen.

Cat walked across the cellar floor and sat down beside him. "Hiya, Rat," he said.

"Hiya, Cat. Pretty dark down here this time of night," Rat said to make small talk. His voice was soft and froggy.

"Pretty dark outside, too," Cat small-talked back. They sat quiet for a while. "Well, what are you thinking about doing tonight, Rat?" Cat asked finally.

"Oh, I did come down here to ask Lady Mouse to go for a walk with me along the River, but she isn't here. She went to the party with Dog."

"Oh," said Cat.

"But I got plenty of other things to do," said Rat real quick.

"Yeah," said Cat, "I know you do." He puffed on his seegar to make the tip of it glow in the dark. "Why don't you go to the party with me, Rat?" he asked. "All the folks will be there, and maybe you could have some fun."

"I suppose," answered Rat.

"I reckon Lady Mouse is there," offered Cat. "Maybe you could talk with her."

Rat looked down at the bulge in his pocket that was the clover flower. "I'm kind of tired of talking to Lady Mouse at the parties, you know what I mean Cat?"

"Yeah, I know what you mean." Cat smoked a while longer. Then he had an idea. "Hey, Rat, you want to go down by the River and chew dandelions and watch the moon rise?"

"Sure," said Rat. "I was just thinking about doing that myself."

"Come on then," said Cat, jumping to his feet and grabbing Rat by the collar of his coat.

"You go on up the stairs, Cat," said Rat, "and I'll catch up with you right after I get some things arranged here."

"Are you really coming?" asked Cat.

"Yes, I am really coming. I just need a couple minutes. I'll catch up."

"All right now, Rat, you better," said Cat, waving his seegar under Rat's nose. Rat nodded his head twice, and Cat climbed the stairs and left him standing on shaky knees in the cellar.

When Cat's tail disappeared from the top step, Rat searched in his pocket for the clover flower. He pulled it out, kind of roughly, so one side of the flower got smashed some, but it still smelled nice. He looked around the dark cellar for a minute, then set the clover flower on Lady Mouse's lamp stand. He knew as soon as he put it there that it was probably a mistake, but he turned and ran up the stairs anyway.

Cat was waiting in the back yard. He was standing on one foot and then the other as he tried to get a splinter out of his tail. He was spitting and fussing. Rat watched him for a while. "What's wrong, Cat?" he asked.

"I got a danged splinter from the stairway in my tail is what's wrong!" yowled Cat. He felt around in his tail fur, but he couldn't find the tip of the splinter. "Rat, will you look for that thing, or am I going to have to go inside and get a needle and the twisters?"

"I'll look," said Rat. He grabbed Cat's tail, and in about two second of looking and poking and prodding and squeezing, he found the splinter and yanked it out.

"EE-ouch!" squawked Cat when Rat yanked. He grabbed his tail out of Rat's paws. "I suppose you got it?"

Rat held up the splinter. It was a long rough one, and it had a drop of Cat's blood on the end.

"Just as I figured," said Cat. "You pulled it out rough side first."

"Well, did you want me to pull it out or not?" huffed Rat, feeling that his good work hadn't been properly thanked.

"Sure, I wanted you to pull it out," said Cat, "but I didn't want you to pull it like a rusty nail from a rotten board! My tail ain't like some leather-whip Rat-tail, you know. Mine's got fur and it's tenderer." Rat pulled his tail behind his legs, feeling embarrassed, but Cat didn't pay any attention. "That's an important thing you ought to be told, Rat, about tails. Not everybody's tail is like that hairless steel-file that you Rats drag around behind you. No sir. Some folks have got nice tails that they use for important things, like keeping their balance when they run or climb, or warming their noses when they sleep out in the cold, or hanging from tree branches, or other stuff like that."

Rat hung his head. "Rats use their tails for stuff…"

"Yeah," snapped Cat, waving his seegar at Rat and really getting wound up in his tail talk, "like tying it into knots when they worry, or poking it into dark holes or corners to find out what's in 'em. No one in his right mind would treat his tail the way a Rat does!" Cat paused for a second and looked at Rat's scarred and beat-up skin-tail. "Of course, no one else has a tail that's as ugly and worthless as a Rat's. Unlike you, Rat, most folks have nice, furry, good-looking tails to lose, so they take better care of them."

Rat almost wished he didn't have a tail. "Well, I kind of like my tail, Cat," he said, holding it up in one paw. Cat looked it over from base to tip, and he felt bad about picking on Rat's tail. Dragging around an awful thing like that his whole life, Rat had enough problems and didn't need Cat pointing it out and making it worse.

"Well, Rat," consoled Cat, "at least you don't have to worry about some fool wanting to cut off your tail and use it for decoration like a Raccoon or a Squirrel does."

"I guess not," agreed Rat. "I guess I got all the luck."

Cat smoothed down his ruffled tail fur a final time. "Let's walk down along the River, Rat," he suggested. "I don't much want to go to another of Dog's parties."

They walked the long way to the River bank, through the pine trees and around the Duck pond. Rat kept looking up at the stars and tripping over roots and bumping into branches. Cat watched him stumble along and he shook his head.

"You sure been acting strange lately, Rat," he said. "You never used to be so clumsy."

"I'll be more careful," promised Rat.

"And you don't eat," scolded Cat.

"I'll eat more," promised Rat.

"And you sit up late and watch the stars all night."

"I'll sleep more," promised Rat.

"And Dog says that you sat with Lady Mouse in the big brown chair at the last party."

"He did?" asked Rat, stopping in the middle of a step over a pine root.

"Yes, he did."

"Oh, my!"

"Did you?" asked Cat.

"What if I did?" asked Rat right back.

"Dog says you told her stories."

"Well, what if I did?"

Cat scratched his head and tried to look at Rat's face in the dark. No one can tell what a Rat is thinking in the dark, not even a Cat. "I don't know what to do, Rat," said Cat. "You feel that way about Lady Mouse, and Dog feels that way about Lady Mouse, and you and me and Dog are supposed to stick together. We spit on it, remember?"

Rat hung his head. "I remember," he said.

"I suppose something will happen," said Cat. "I don't know what it is, but something is sure to happen." The moon rose over the hills on the far side of the River, and they stood quiet in the moonshadows of the pine trees. Then Rat sighed a sad little sigh, and they walked on.

When they reached the bank of the River the moon was already high in the night sky, and they could see its reflection on the slow-moving water. There was a big patch of dandelions on the bank, and they walked into the middle of it. They each pulled some dandelion stems to chew while they looked up at the moon and stars in the midnight sky.

Cat and Rat were both good dandelion chewers. They picked only the ones that still had some white fluff on the top, and they were careful to tear them off just above the wilted leaves without mashing the stem closed. When they both had their paws full of stems, they walked out onto a narrow finger of the bank that jutted out into the River. They lay back in the thick grass with their heads propped up so that they could see the stars and the moon up in the sky and the same stars and moon reflected in the smooth water of the River.

Holding the dandelion stems straight up, they would suck the juice out of them. It isn't easy to do. You have to practice a long time to learn how to get all of the sweet inside-stem juice without getting too much of the bitter outside-stem juice.

"These are good dandelions," Rat said, squeezing a drop of juice from the purple end of a stem.

"Pretty good," agreed Cat, "but they were better before the first frost. Now they're a mite bitter."

"Maybe so," said Rat, "but there's nothing else I'd rather be doing tonight."

"Me too," Cat said with a happy smile. Rat didn't see that happy Cat-smile very often. It was nice.

A pool of oil came floating down the River, and when it was right in front of Cat and Rat it made the reflection of the moon change into seven different colors like a round rainbow.

"Pretty," said Cat.

"Yeah, pretty," said Rat.

"No, it ain't pretty!" said a deep, gruff voice. Rat almost choked on his dandelion stem, and Cat tried to jump up so fast that one foot slipped into the River and got wet and cold. "It most certainly ain't pretty. Not pretty at all," said the gruff voice again. Cat and Rat looked behind them and saw it was a Beaver sitting on the River bank. He was smoking a corncob pipe. "Chewing dandelions, huh?" the Beaver asked Cat and Rat.

"Yep," said Rat.

"Well, you're welcome to chew all you want, but it's an odd thing to do. Mighty odd," said Beaver.

"Come sit with us a while," offered Rat. "You can chew a few of my dandelions, if you want."

"No thanks," said Beaver. "I'll just sit here and smoke my pipe." Cat sniffed the smoke curling out of Beaver's corncob pipe. It was corn-silk smoke. Beaver was smoking corn silk. Now that's an odd thing to do, thought Cat. He looked again at the pool of oil on the water, shimmering in different colors.

"I think it's pretty," Cat said to Beaver. "Why do you say it ain't pretty?"

"Because it ain't natural," said Beaver. "The moon's natural color is white, or sometimes orange when it's rising on a fall night and the corn and pumpkins are ripe. But it should never be the unnatural colors it gets from bad stuff floating down the River." Beaver tapped the ashes from his pipe and put it into his coat pocket. He sat with his big front paws on his knees and looked at the River with sad eyes. "You know what makes the moon's reflection them colors?" he asked nobody in particular.

"No," answered Rat.

"Unnatural stuff that's been dumped into the water," Beaver said with a little nod toward the pool of oil, now sliding out of sight father down the River.

"Unnatural stuff?" asked Cat. "What do you mean 'unnatural stuff'?"

"Oh, oil and trash and sewage and garbage and poison and chemicals and everything else that People decide they want to throw away," said Beaver. "Dumping unnatural stuff into the River might not mean much to you City folks," said Beaver, "but around here it's the most important bad thing that has ever happened. Nobody wants to live where unnatural stuff is in the water. Almost all the turtles are gone, the frogs don't do nothing but bellyache, and most of the fish have left, except for the bottom sludgers and the muck snails."

Cat and Rat and Beaver sat quiet on the bank as another pool of oil slid across the reflection of the moon on the River.

"I'm just about the last of the old River folks that are still here," said Beaver. "It won't be long before no one can live here, except for the Rats." Rat gave Beaver a sideways look, and Beaver noticed for the first time that Rat was a Rat. "And you're welcome to it," said Beaver. "Nobody else can live here anyway. It's just a shame what they've done."

"Who done?" asked Cat.

"Why, the People!" said Beaver. "They do all the unnatural stuff." He sniffed. "Pretty soon, I ain't going to have a home on the River anymore because of the People."

"Because of all the unnatural stuff they dump in the River?" asked Cat.

"No. Because they are going to tear down my dam."

"Why?" asked Rat. It made him a little angry.

"To build a bridge for the new road," said Beaver. "My dam is a good dam, too. Keeps the River just right for everyone. Not too fast, not too slow. Not too deep, not too shallow. Not too narrow, not too wide. But they are going to tear down my natural dam, build an unnatural dam right where it is now, and put a road bridge over the top of it. I don't think this new dam will be as good as mine, even if it does hold a new road."

"What new road?" asked Cat.

"Oh, just another big road they are building for more People to drive on and come to the River and spoil it," said Beaver. "They'll put up this new unnatural dam to try to fix the River so it can be crossed by a bridge for the new road. But an unnatural dam never fixes anything. It always spoils everything. This new dam won't be as good as my old dam. It won't work right. They never do."

"Who told you about this new road?" asked Cat.

"Everybody knows about it," said Beaver. He pointed toward the Three-Story House. "This new road they are building will run from the old road by the Dump, across the River on a bridge, and go right through that old house. That's why nobody lives there anymore.

"It's going to spoil everything, you just wait and see. Everything along this part of the River will be ruined. Nobody will be able to stay." Beaver sniffed again and dug into his coat pocket to find his corncob pipe.

"Maybe they won't do it," said Cat. "Maybe they won't build the dam and the bridge and the road."

"Yes, they will," said Beaver sadly. "I know these People." He stuffed his pipe full of corn silk, lit it with a match, and took a couple puffs. "People come and spoil everything until you have to leave." He looked through the cloud of pipe smoke toward the River. "I don't want to leave," he said. "I want to stay. I've stayed here a long, long time.

"I stayed when the floods came and washed out everything on the River bank. I stayed when the tornado blew down half the trees. I stayed when the ice storm broke down the rest. I stayed though the coldest winters and the hottest summers. I stayed and I stayed through all sorts of hard times and good times for a whole life here on the River. But I won't be able to stay though this. I know these People."

"Where will you go?' asked Rat.

"I don't know where to go," answered Beaver. "I ain't got nowhere to go. I don't want to go nowhere. I just wanted to stay here a while longer."

Beaver smoked his pipe, and they sat and watched the River flow by and the moon get higher and higher in the night sky until its reflection disappeared from the water. Rat was glad it was gone, because each time some unnatural stuff in the water floated by and made the reflection change to some strange color he felt awful. Beaver stood up and stretched.

"I got to be going, folks," he said. "I'm sorry if I interrupted your dandelion chewing and River watching. Bad times are coming, and I hope you have better luck than me."

"So long, Beaver," said Cat. "I hope you have some better luck, too."

"Luck's not for me," answered Beaver, shaking his head. "All my luck was here, and pretty soon all this will be spoiled." He waddled down to the River bank and swam away.

"I don't want to chew any more dandelions," said Rat. "My tummy hurts."

"Let's go home," said Cat. He helped Rat to his feet and they walked back through the pine trees. Cat was thinking all the while.

"How can a road go over a Dump, Rat?" he asked. "How can a road bridge go over a dam? How can a road go right through a nice, big house? How can all that happen? I don't think a road can do that, Rat."

"I hope not," said Rat, "because if it does, what would we do?"

They stopped at the edge of the yard of the Three-Story House and listened to the sounds of the party dying down.

"Let's go sit by the fireplace, Rat," said Cat. "I got to think about this. I go to think about what we can do."

"Okay, you do the thinking for us, Cat," said Rat. "You'll figure something out."

Chapter 10
The Road Machine

Smack in the middle of the front yard was a Road Machine. It was almost as big as the Three-Story House. While everyone was sleeping, it had rolled right up to the front porch on its steel-and-rubber caterpillar tracks. It had torn up big hunks of grass and dirt from the yard and scattered them everywhere. It was a terrible, horrible, awful, scary machine.

On the front of the Road Machine were the smasher, the crusher, and the grinder, and above them were two big headlights that looked like monster eyes. In the middle of the Road Machine were the leveler and the smoother, and at the back was the paver. Each of the parts was as big as a truck, and they were full of steel teeth and gears and burners and rollers and pounders.

Wherever it went, the Road Machine destroyed everything in front of it and left a road behind it. It ate up and chewed up and spit out anything that got in its way. Now the Three-Story House was in its way.

Fool Owl had seen the Road Machine first when he was drinking breakfast tea and looked out the front window. He dropped his teacup and it broke on the floor with a clink and a crash. Owl woke Dog, and he had a look at the Road Machine. Dog woke Lady Mouse, and she had a look at it. Lady Mouse woke Bluebird, and when she had a look at the Road Machine she woke everyone else in the whole house.

"Help! Help! Help!" Bluebird screeched as she ran up and down the stairs and through every room, flapping her wings and dropping feathers behind her. "It's come to get us! That thing has come to get us! It's going to get us all!"

Cat woke up like a lightning bolt wanting to strike. "What?" he yowled as he grabbed Bluebird by the tail. "What thing? What's going to get us?"

"That thing! That thing in the front yard!" screamed Bluebird. "We haven't got a chance!"

"And me with a headache," moaned Rat from the corner of the front room, pulling his blanket up to his eyes and wishing he had not drunk two cans of wassel when he got home last night.

All the folks were crowded around the front room windows staring out at the Road Machine. Cat shouldered his way through the crowd and looked it over carefully.

"When did it get into the front yard?" Cat asked.

"No one could possibly know," said Fool Owl. "It crept in there in the dark of night when no one was aware. It must be as stealthy and sneaky as a Cat."

Cat gave Fool Owl a sour look.

"That's the trouble with wassel parties," said Dog. "You find such terrible things on the morning after."

"We've got to investigate this," said Cat. "I'm going to go out there and check it over."

"You can't! You can't!" twittered Bluebird. "If you go out there, it will get you!"

Cat took a seegar out of his coat pocket, lit it, puffed on it twice, and gave Bluebird his tired old stare. "Bluebird," he asked, "can a Road Machine move without People to operate it?"

Bluebird shrugged her shoulders to show that she didn't know if it could.

"No, you featherhead, it cannot," said Cat. "And do you, Bluebird, or anybody else, think there are any People around that machine?"

Everybody shrugged their shoulders to show that they didn't know what to think.

"Well, I got eyes, and my eyes don't see any People around that machine, so I don't think it is going to get me if I go out there, Bluebird," Cat sassed her, which was not a nice thing to do when she was so scared. She smoothed her feathers and said she knew it was safe all along and was never really worried and knew Cat would take care of things.

Cat turned up his coat collar, opened the front door, and walked out onto the porch. All the folks followed him out, one-by-one, walking slowly. "Maybe we can do something about this," muttered Cat to himself as he walked around the machine, looking at every part of it, and thinking this was the biggest and most horrible thing he had ever seen in his life.

Rat was still inside the house, watching Cat and the Road Machine from behind a front room window. He remembered what Beaver had told them the night before, and he didn't believe that Cat could do anything to save the Three-Story House now. Lady Mouse walked by, and Rat grabbed her by the tail.

"Really, Rat!" she huffed as she pulled her tail away and gave him a slap on the paw.

Rat's face turned red from the tip of his nose to the tops of his ears. "I'm sorry, Lady Mouse, but I have to talk to you," he said. "It's about something awfully important."

"What is it now?" asked Lady Mouse with a sniff and a flip of her head.

"I can't talk to you here," pleaded Rat. "Come to the kitchen with me and I'll fix you a bowl of tea while I explain it to you."

"A cup of tea, Rat," said Lady Mouse. "Proper folks drink tea from a cup, not from a bowl."

"Well, a cup of tea then," said Rat as he took her by the paw and led her to the kitchen.

Out in the yard, Cat had picked up a good, sturdy stick and was whacking and smacking the Road Machine every which way. With each smack or whack, everyone moved back a step, expecting the Road Machine to get him, but it didn't budge. It just sat there silent and never moved an inch.

"Get away from here, Road Machine!" yowled Cat. "Yellow…" SMACK! "Dirty…" WHACK! "Ugly…" SMACK! "Nasty…" WHACK! "Road Machine!" He was pretty soon tuckered out from all the smacking and whacking and yakking, and he sat down right in front of the Road Machine and glared into its smasher and crusher and grinder.

"Must you sit there, Cat?" asked Fool Owl. "You never know when it might wake up hungry. I've heard that one of these Road Machines ate a garbage truck once, and it didn't even spit out the bones."

"Did you ever think, Owl," chided Cat, "that I might get hungry and eat that dirty yellow machine?"

Fool Owl thought for a moment, then shook his head. "No, Cat. I never thought that."

Cat sat still and quiet for a long, long time. Folks began to fidget and worry.

"What will we do, Cat?" asked Chipmunk.

Cat didn't say a word. He didn't make a sound.

"What should we do, Cat?" asked Skunk.

Cat didn't answer.

"Are you going to make a deal with it, Cat?" asked Crow.

"Do you have some definite plan of action that we might follow?" asked Owl.

Cat sat still and silent. He didn't move even a whisker. He didn't even blink an eye. First one, and then a few, and then all of the folks walked back into the Three-Story House and left Cat alone in the front yard with the Road Machine. He stared into the headlights. He glared at the smasher, the crusher, the grinder, the leveler, the smoother, the paver. He looked at the big steel-and-rubber caterpillar tracks. Then he stared into the headlights again. They were still staring back at him.

At last Cat stood up and shook his head. For the very first time in his whole life, he didn't know what to do. He reared back and threw the big stick all the way over the top of the Road Machine's staring headlight eyes. It hit with a CLANK! on the far side, but the Road Machine never blinked. Cat hung his head and walked back into the Three-Story House by himself.

The House was as quiet as the day that Dog and Cat and Rat had first walked into it. Folks were moving around, here and there, upstairs and down, packing to leave, not making a sound. Crow was putting his black stovepipe top hat into a hat box that was too small. Chipmunk was rolling all his spare clothes and paper clip collection into a red bandana. Bluebird was laying out all her dress feathers side-by-side.

Cat was feeling sadder than he had ever felt. Then he saw Dog sitting in the big brown chair and looking even sadder. Cat stepped over Bluebird's feathers and put his arm around Dog's shoulders. Dog looked up, and a tear ran down his nose and dripped off the end.

"It's just terrible, Cat," sniffed Dog.

Cat nodded his head. "That danged yellow Road Machine!" he said.

"No!" moaned Dog. "Not that. It's Rat."

"Rat?" snapped Cat. "What's happened to Rat?"

"It ain't what happened to him that's terrible," said Dog. "It's what he did that's terrible." Another tear rolled out of his eye.

"What did he do?"

"He asked Lady Mouse to go to the City with him," sniffled Dog.

Cat nodded his head once, real slowly.

"Do you think she will, Cat?" asked Dog.

"Will what?"

"Go back to the City with Rat."

"I don't know, Dog. Maybe. Maybe not."

"It's just terrible, Cat," moaned Dog. "Just terrible."

"Where is Rat now?" asked Cat.

"Packing," sniffed Dog.

"Where is Lady Mouse?"

"She's packing, too."

Cat nodded again.

"It doesn't look good, does it Cat?"

"It doesn't look anything yet," answered Cat. "Go get you and me cups of tea while I think this all out."

Dog got out of the chair and dragged off toward the kitchen like it was a two-mile walk on a hot day. Cat sat in the brown chair and tried to think. The Rabbits were on the floor by the fireplace divvying up their bottle caps, and their chatter was driving Cat crazy. Just when he started to figure things out, someone tugged at his sleeve. It was Lady Mouse.

"Please give this letter to the Rat," she said to Cat in her snippiest voice, holding out a pink and white sheet of paper that was folded small.

"Where is Rat?" asked Cat.

"I certainly wouldn't know," answered Lady Mouse.

"Ain't you leaving with him to go to the City?" asked Cat.

"Aren't, not ain't. That's the proper language to use," said Lady Mouse.

Cat lit a seegar and puffed on it while he waited for Lady Mouse to wise up.

"Well, I'm not," she said at last.

"Not what?" asked Cat.

"Not going to the City with Rat."

Cat took the letter from her and put it into his coat pocket. "Well, wherever you're going, so long, Mouse." Cat blew a cloud of smoke in her direction. Lady Mouse picked up her suitcase and marched out through the front door in a huff.

Cat tried to think about the Road Machine, but he couldn't because he kept thinking about Dog and Rat. So he tried to think about Dog and Rat, but he couldn't because he kept thinking about the Road Machine. It wasn't long before his thinking was all twisted into knots. He wished Dog would come back with a cup of hot tea. Instead, Rat walked into the front room with his coat pockets stuffed full and a worried look on his face. He was twitching his tail back and forth and being a nervous Rat. He saw Cat sitting in the brown chair and edged over to talk to him.

"Cat," he whispered, "I can't find Lady Mouse anywhere."

"Rat…"

"I've asked everyone if they have seen her or know where she is, but they are all so busy packing to leave that they haven't noticed her."

"Rat…" Cat tried again.

"Fool Owl said he doesn't have the slightest notion where she is. None of the third floor birds know, either. Not even the junk Mice have seen her, and…"

"Rat!" yowled Cat.

"What?" asked Rat, looking hurt.

"I've been trying to tell you three times that I've got something to tell you."

"Well, just tell it to me, Cat. Don't sit there jabbering about it!"

Cat could see that Rat was real upset, so he let his smart-talk pass. He reached into his pocket, snapped out the letter from Lady Mouse, and held it in front of Rat's nose. Rat flinched and shut his eyes. When he opened them again, Cat popped him on the end of his nose with the sharp edge of the letter. Rat yelled like he was stung by a bee and grabbed his nose with both front paws as he fell onto his fat behind. Cat flipped the letter into Rat's lap and sat back to relight his seegar.

"Whash thish?' asked Rat through his paws.

"A letter to you," said Cat.

"From who?" asked Rat.

"Lady Mouse," replied Cat as if he didn't care, although he really did.

"Oh," said Rat. He sat there looking at the folded-up letter for a while, then he opened it and pressed out all the folds and creases and wrinkles against the breast of his coat. He laid it out all square on the floor and played with the corners of it.

"Ain't you going to read it?" Cat asked him when he couldn't stand any more of Rat's letter fooling and fussing.

"I can't read very good, Cat. You know that," mumbled Rat, looking down at the floor.

"Oh," said Cat.

"Maybe that's why Lady Mouse never did take to me, Cat, on account of I can't read and write and all them fancy things."

Cat looked at him like he was the stupidest Rat in the world.

"It figures in a way," continued Rat, "because there's lots of things she probably likes to do – like reading and writing and so forth – that I can't do. What do you think about that, Cat?"

"Do you want me to read the letter to you, Rat?" asked Cat.

Rat thought about it for a minute. "I guess so," he said. He picked up the letter and looked at it one more time. Then he handed it to Cat.

Cat took it and turned it top edge up. He cleared his throat and was trying to read the first words when he saw Bluebird standing by his elbow. She was leaning in closer for a better listen.

"This letter is personal," Cat growled at Bluebird.

Rat's nose turned cold. "How personal is it, Cat?" he asked, getting ready to snatch it back.

"Too personal for any featherhead to hear," said Cat.

"Well, I never!" cheeped Bluebird as she took a step back and ruffled her feathers.

"You mean you tried but you never," Cat sassed her and blew a puff of smoke her way. She picked up her package of fine feathers and her handbag and hopped angrily out the front door without looking back. Cat flipped out the letter and started reading again.

"It says here, 'Dear Rat...'"

"Will you just read it straight, Cat!" chided Rat who was too nervous and fidgety to sit still and listen.

"I am just reading it straight!" yowled Cat. He bit down hard on the stump of his seegar, muttered a few words under his breath, and then cleared his throat again.

"It says:"

Dear Rat,

After thinking too much about our recent talk when we discussed you and I and Dog and what will happen now that we are all leaving the Three-Story House, I have decided not to go to the City with you, or even see you at all since you don't know anything right.

I think it was mean of you to say that I and everyone else is fighting for some of Dog's attention and love, like folks fighting for the biggest piece of pie. In fact, Dog has lots of attention and love to give everyone, like a never-empty bottle of blueberry soda, so no one ever has to go thirsty.

Thus, I do believe we should never see each other again, since you say I must choose either you or Dog, and I would never, ever be able to hurt poor Dog that way.

So I do not want you to come and visit me, ever, and especially not tomorrow at three o'clock, at the piano box on the south side of the Dump, which is where I am moving and will be living alone for the next several days or more.

Sincerely,

Lady Mouse

"Is that all it says?" asked Rat.

"Well," answered Cat as he peered at the letter, "it says N.R.S.V.P. at the very bottom of the page."

"What does N.R.S.V.P. mean?" asked Rat, wrinkling up his face.

"I ain't sure," said Cat. "No Rats Should Visit Please, I guess."

Rat took the letter from Cat, folded it, put it into his inside coat pocket, and stood up. He didn't know what he should do. Finally, he started walking toward the kitchen.

"Where you going, Fat Rat?" Cat hollered after him.

"I think I'll walk down to the River," answered Rat. He went out the kitchen door just as Dog was coming in with two cups of hot tea. They looked at each other with real sad eyes. Then Rat was gone.

"Here's your tea, Cat," said Dog. He took a big gulp of his own. It tasted bitter. Cat took a little sip from his cup, but he didn't want to drink any tea right now.

"Is Lady Mouse leaving with Rat?" Dog asked. His eyes were dry but he was still sniffly.

"No," said Cat. "She went to live in the piano box on the south side of the Dump."

"Where did Rat go?"

"I don't know," said Cat, "but I don't think he's coming back."

The two of them sat together not drinking tea for the longest time. All the folks were leaving with their sacks and bundles and packages and suitcases and travel bags. It took most of the day for everyone to move out. Chipmunk stopped to say good-bye, and Crow left them each a business card, but most just wandered off without saying a word. As the evening light got dim, Cat and Dog were alone in the Three-Story House.

"What will you do now, Cat?" asked Dog.

"Probably go back to the City. What about you?"

"First, I'm going to the Dump to talk with Lady Mouse," said Dog. "After that, I don't know."

"It's getting pretty late in the day," said Cat. "Maybe you should get started."

"Yep," said Dog. He climbed out of the chair and brushed off his pants and coat with his paws. Then he pushed back the curly hair on his head and blew his nose on a green handkerchief. "I'm on my way," he said.

"Ain't you going to pack?" asked Cat.

"I don't need to take anything," said Dog. "I'll get other stuff whenever I get to where I'm going. So long, Cat. See you in the City."

"So long, Dog."

Dog left the front door wide open when he went out. Night was coming on, and Cat didn't feel like sitting in a dark, empty house. He walked to the front window and took his last seegar and a box of matches from an inside coat pocket. The Road Machine was in the front yard, staring at Cat with its big headlight eyes.

"Dang machine," growled Cat. He struck a match to light his seegar and watched the reflection of the flame glow in the glass of the window. And for the first time that day, he knew exactly what he was going to do.

Chapter 11
Fire And Farewell

Dog was sleeping on top of a pile of tin cans at the Dump when smoke blew into his nose. He sat up with a jerk. He was sleepy, but not too sleepy to chase a fire truck if one should come by. Over the edge of the pit he could see an orange glow in the sky that looked like a sunrise, but it was midnight. Dog walked up to the rim of the garbage pit and he saw, far away, that the Three-Story House was right in the middle of that soft orange-and-yellow glow, and off to one side was a dark shadow sitting on a hill. It was Cat!

Dog stretched and shook himself and wobbly-walked up the hill toward Cat to get a better look at what was happening. The glow around the Three-Story House was getting bigger and bigger and brighter and brighter. Cat heard him coming and looked at Dog over his shoulder.

"Hiya, Dog-ears!" he shouted with a happy smile.

Dog rubbed his eyes and sat down beside Cat. "What's going on?" he asked.

"See for yourself!"

Dog took a closer look and saw that the orange glow was flames of fire, and those flames were slowly crawling up the sides of the Three-Story House. "Fire! Fire!" he howled. "Some fire!"

"You betcha," said Cat with a nod. He held up a big paper bag. "You want to split these with me?"

"Sure," said Dog. "What are they?"

"Marshmallows."

Dog opened the bag, took out a marshmallow, and popped it into his mouth. "They're kind of hard," he said after a couple chomps.

"Don't eat them now," said Cat. "We'll roast them later over the hot coals of the fire and they'll be fine."

They watched the Three-Story House burn. It was a terrible fire, one of the best that Dog had ever seen. Earlier, before the smoke had awakened Dog, the fire had started down in the cellar, come up through the floor of the kitchen, and gone curling out the windows to set the sides of the house ablaze. As they watched, the paint turned black on the outside of the second and third floors, all the way to the roof. Then with a POOF! and a ROAR! all the walls burst into flames and the whole house was wrapped in fire. It burned steadily until all the windows cracked and fell out, and then it flared high and spread to the roof. Fingers of fire reached around the front porch, and soon it was smoking and creaking.

"I wish we could see the back of the house," said Cat. "Something big and awful is probably happening there, and we'll never know what it is."

"Plenty of awful stuff is happening here at the front side," said Dog, watching the fire burn higher and higher and higher right before his wide eyes. "Did you see how the shingles curled up and melted when the fire came through the roof?"

The whole Three-Story House was burning wild and fiery, so hot and bright that Cat and Dog could hardly look at it without shading their eyes. Hundred-foot flames shot into the night sky with a WHOOSH! and a BOOM! as sections of the roof buckled and fell inside. Sparks and embers were showering down, making little fires that speckled the front yard.

Gaping holes opened in the walls as the flames inside the house ate through them, and Cat and Dog saw that every room inside the house was full of raging, terrible fire and smoke. Ceiling beams cracked in the heat and collapsed into the heart of the fire with a screeching-screaming CRASH! and the house began to slump in on itself.

"Now comes the real excitement!" yowled Cat, poking Dog in the ribs with his elbow.

The biggest brick chimney leaned slowly, slowly forward as the walls of the house caved in. The fire seemed to burn low as the chimney fell silently down, down, down and out across the front room, and then shattered into a million red-hot bricks that smashed onto the porch and the yard with a rolling RUMBLE! so loud that Dog and Cat put their paws over their ears. A fiery wave of broken bricks and coals poured across the porch, and with a MOAN! and a SNAP! the porch broke away from the house in a ball of flames that swept right over the Road Machine!

The fire sank to a whisper as smoking boards and hot bricks tumbled off the top of the Road Machine and clanked onto its smasher and crusher and grinder and leveler and smoother and paver and its steel-and-rubber caterpillar tracks. Its monster headlight eyes never blinked as they poked out of the flames and smoke and smoldering coals. For a moment, Cat thought that not even the end of the world could stop that awful machine. Then he heard it groan.

A sheet of scorched yellow metal on the hood of the smasher twisted up and away from the fire below, and the Road Machine groaned again, louder this time. Waves of heat made scorch streaks of red and black along the sides of the crusher and the grinder. Plastic knobs and handles melted and oozed down in smears that started to smoke and then to burn. The operator's seat caught fire. The rubber joints on one caterpillar track split and broke, and the track fell off its drive wheels and into the fire.

The Cat heard a POP! and he saw the cap of the fuel tank flip open at the back of the machine. Boiling hot gasoline spewed out of the tank, ran down into the paver that was full of oil and tar, and burst into flames.

Fire exploded two hundred feet high from the Road Machine, burning so bright that it almost made the house disappear! Metal shrieked and squealed as fire scorched and twisted and wrenched and ruined it. Hoses and belts and wires caught fire, making lines of flame through the machine from end to end. Black oily smoke blotted out half the sky as fire boiled and rolled through the paver, and fiery tar flowed into the smoother and the leveler and reached forward to burn the grinder and the crusher and the smasher. The whole Road Machine was wrapped in flames hotter than a blast furnace, hotter than a volcano, hotter than the fires of hell. A wall of heat swept across the hill, wilting the grass and making Dog and Cat cover their faces with their coats and wonder if they were going to burn to a crisp.

The fire inside the Three-Story House had died down, but now it began to roar louder and louder as the screams from the burning Road Machine shrilled higher and higher. The house leaned farther and farther forward, looming over the Road Machine, until those two big fires became one great enormous fire! Then with a sigh, the Three-Story House toppled onto the Road Machine and swept across the yard and spread out until it was a huge pool of low flames with a melting steel lump at the center. The fire muttered and spit and grumbled as it ate the last of the scraps, everything that could it burn or melt.

Dog and Cat sat shaking on the hilltop. Their fur was scorched and their eyes ached from the smoke and the heat. Dog tried to swallow, but his mouth was too dry and tasted like ashes. Cat felt sick in his stomach from the smell of burning tar and oil. Now that the heat of the fire was not blowing over them, they felt freezing cold. They huddled together and watched small bursts of flames pop up here and there in the fiery pool. Neither said a word through the rest of that long night as the ruins of the Three-Story House and the Road Machine burned down to coals. At last the light of the sunrise faded the glow of the fire.

"I'm going down there," Cat said in a croaky voice. "I've got to see it close-up."

Dog nodded. "I'll come too."

They walked to the edge of the yard, which was all burned black and grimy. They found sticks and started poking and prodding in the ashes. Cat had never seen a fire that left so little. One glass headlight eye from the Road Machine looked up at him from under a smoldering porch board. Cat tapped it with his stick and it broke into three pieces. There was nothing left but shards and slivers and cinders and soot. A handle was sticking up from a pile of coals, and Dog hooked onto it with his stick and pulled. It was the cast iron skillet from the kitchen stove, red hot.

"That's just what we need," said Dog. He set it level on two hot rocks, then reached into his coat pocket and took out four fresh eggs. He cracked them into the skillet and tossed the shells into the embers. "How do you want yours cooked, Cat?"

Cat saw those eggs sizzling in the skillet, and a big grin started to grow on his face. The grin turned into a smile, the smile turned into a giggle, the giggle turned into a belly laugh, and he had to sit down before it got the best of him. "How do I want them cooked? Lookin' at me! That's how I want them cooked, you Scrawny Dog." He wiped the laugh tears from his eyes. "Sunny side up and lookin' at me."

"That's best," agreed Dog. "Sunny side up and lookin' at both of us."

Some of the Three-Story House folks had seen the fire's light during the night, and now they came wandering back to see what it was all about. Cat and Dog wouldn't talk about it. "No questions, please," said Dog.

Chipmunk had a loaf of bread, and he laid slices of it into the hot skillet to make toast for everyone. Weasel had a jar of grape jam. Crow and Fool Owl walked all the way around the fire wreckage, peering into it here and there, and Owl told everyone he knew exactly what happened, although he really didn't know anything at all. He-Otter and She-Otter leaned against each other and whispered in secret. The Rabbits searched for souvenirs.

Fool Owl waited until everyone was gathered together, and then he commenced to preach. "Now what will become of us?" he asked no one in particular. "Ruin and destruction has come upon us. All, all the good, worthy, friendly folks who once lived in this fine house – all lost in the fire of retribution."

"Who?" asked Chipmunk.

"Sweet Bluebird, for one," said Owl.

"I'm right here," chirped Bluebird.

Fool Owl looked around. "Well then, Skunk. Skunk that wonderful fellow who was generous and giving and loved by us all. He's gone."

"Skunk is down by the River, catching fish for breakfast," said Weasel.

"And the Rabbits. The poor, helpless, fun-loving Rabbits," sobbed Owl.

"We're over here, toasting Cat's marshmallows on a stick," hollered one of the Rabbits.

"The junk Mice…"

"…have all gone to live at the Dump," said Chipmunk.

"And of course the petite and beautiful Lady Mouse," said Owl. He took a tissue from his sleeve, blew his nose and went on mourning. "What will become of us now? What of the respected Monsignor Cat? The beloved Brother Dog? Humble Fat Rat? Kindly Crow? The birds, those many and various strange birds? Oh, I could go on and on."

"Please don't!" yowled Cat.

"Everyone will be fine, just fine," Bluebird soothed Fool Owl and gave him a pat on the back.

"Such tragedy," wept Owl. "Such heartless tragedy. Such wonderful tragedy."

Cat rolled his eyes away from Fool Owl, and who should he see walking towards him from the Dump? Rat! He grabbed Dog's tail, gave it a yank, and pointed. Dog saw Rat, too, and they both left their breakfast to go talk with him.

Rat was a sight. He had a navy blue stocking cap on his head and a knapsack over his shoulder. He was wearing a baggy brown sweater, leather work gloves, gray wool pants and black knee boots that were laced up tight. His coat was gone, but he had a box of seegars and a pack of matches sticking out of one back pocket of his pants. Cat could see that he was ready to do some serious traveling.

"Why are you all dressed up in those new clothes, Rat?" asked Dog.

"These are traveling clothes," said Rat. "I'm traveling far. Leaving today. Right now, as a matter of fact."

"Where are you going?" asked Cat.

"I don't know for sure," said Rat, shifting the knapsack to his other shoulder. Cat could see it was heavy. "I'll head down the River and see where it takes me."

"This River goes to a bigger River, and then to the Sea," said Dog. "I saw a picture of it in a book once."

"Well, the Sea is a good place for a Rat," said Rat. "I know lots of Rats that went to Sea and sailed off to find their fortunes."

"In ships," said Dog.

"Yep, in ships," agreed Rat. Rat and Dog were making small talk without looking straight at each other. They only had one thing to talk about, really, and neither one could talk about it. But Cat could.

"What about Lady Mouse?" Cat asked Rat.

Rat turned to Cat with a funny-faced look. "Oh, I don't care for her no more, Cat," he said. "Now that the Three-Story House is gone. I don't think she would like to travel, so there's no use in me asking her."

Cat nodded, but he looked at a bulge that was in Rat's sweater, and he knew it was the letter from Lady Mouse. It was next to Rat's heart, and on the outside of his sweater he had pinned a white clover flower. Rat saw Cat looking at the clover flower, and he covered it with one paw.

"I got to be on my way," he said. "Morning's the best time of day for traveling." He pulled his stocking cap down tight on his head and hitched up his knapsack. "Take care of yourselves," he said. He stepped forward and gave Cat a big hug, and then he put his arm around Dog and gave him a little hug, too. Dog kind of stiffened up at first, but then he gave Rat a little hug back.

"So long, Rat," said Dog.

"Watch after your luck, Rat," said Cat.

"I will," answered Rat. "I'm going to be a smarter Rat from now on. Smarter. Smarr-tter." He trudged off toward the River, stopped and turned to wave good-bye to Dog and Cat, then disappeared into the grove of pine trees.

Cat had a lump in his stomach and didn't want any more breakfast. Dog ate the rest of their eggs and toast. All the folks were gone, even the Rabbits, and Cat and Dog watched the last of the fire burn down and go cold.

"What will you do now, Dog?" asked Cat.

"Go back to the City, I reckon," answered Dog.

"What about Lady Mouse?"

Dog got the same funny-faced look that Cat had seen on Rat's face. "I don't know," Dog said with a shrug of his shoulders. "I guess I will say good-bye to her when I go through the Dump and past the piano box. I don't think she would like a Dog's life in the City."

Cat shook his head. He just couldn't understand. What was it all about? Dog stood up and brushed back his curly ears. "Time for me to be leaving," he said. He grabbed Cat around the neck and gave him a double-hard hug. "Maybe I'll see you in the City sometime."

"Sure," said Cat. "We'll see each other in the City, probably." He was going to say more, but Dog was walking away fast toward the Dump, so he just waved good-bye. Dog waved back. "So long, Cat!" he hollered.

"So long, Dog."

Well, thought Cat, I've got all day to walk back to the City. He reached into his coat pocket to find a seegar and a box of matches, but the only things in there were a brass button from Fat Rat's old tattered coat and Scrawny Dog's automatic pipe lighter.

"I'll be danged," Cat muttered to himself. "I wonder why I kept those?" He went to toss them into the ashes and soot of the Three-Story House, but he couldn't do it. He looked at that button and that pipe lighter, squeezed them tight in his paw, and put them back into his coat pocket carefully.

Because they were all he had left from happier days.

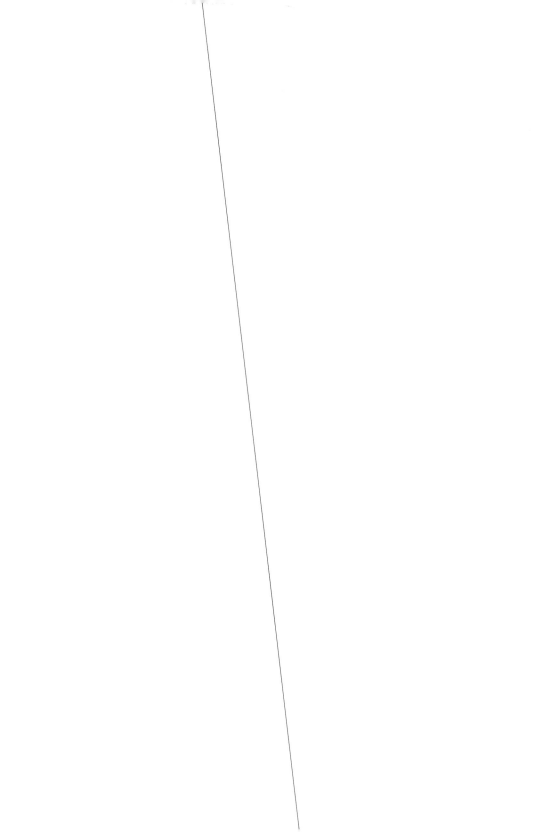

Made in the USA
San Bernardino, CA
28 June 2014